Reimagining the California Missions

A Former Franciscan Friar's Search for the Truth

Mark R. Day

Reimagining the California Missions
© 2025 copyright Mark R. Day

front cover artwork:
https://commons.wikimedia.org/wiki/File:Mission_San_Carlos_
Borromeo_de_Carmelo_%28Oriana_Day,_c.1877%E2%80%9384%29.jpg

https://citizendium.org/wiki/File:Don_Fernando_
Rivera_violates_Church_asylum.png

back cover artwork:
https://en.m.wikipedia.org/wiki/File:Mission_San_Jose_natives.jpg

https://commons.wikimedia.org/wiki/File:The_Spanish_in_
the_Southwest_%281903%29_%2814595481907%29.jpg

Editorial and design functions provided by
Linden Publishing, Fresno, California

ISBN: 979-8-218-61879-7

Printed in the United States of America

praise for *Reimagining the California Missions*

"Mark Day's gripping memoir-history of the Spanish missions brings the perspective of a former Franciscan priest to a topic that matters urgently for all Californians today. How should the missions and their difficult history be told and remembered? Mark weaves together his own autobiography with an account of the painful history of the missions. Here readers will learn something about themselves and something important about our state."

—Jennifer S. Hughes, Department of History,
University of California, Riverside

"Award-winning journalist, author, and documentary filmmaker Mark Day's . . . splendid work tackles the unvarnished story of the Spanish conquest of and oft-brutal treatment of the region's indigenous people. *Reimagining the California Missions* is an important contribution to the annals of California—and America itself."

—Peter F. Stevens, *New York Times* bestselling author
and contributing editor to *Boston Irish Magazine*

"Mark Day recognizes his obligation to tell the truth, and he does so side by side with the Native tribes of California."

—Valentin Lopez, Chairman, Amah Mutsun
tribal band of Central California

"That Mark Day is a former Franciscan friar makes his concise book *Reimagining the California Missions* all the more remarkable. Having seen the light regarding the sins and abuses of the California Catholic mission system, Day includes his understanding of the horrific Doctrine of Christian Domination, which was unleashed on the planet by the wizardry of various popes of the Catholic Church and imposed on original nations and peoples across the planet."

—Steven T. Newcomb, author of *Pagans in the Promised Land: Decoding the Doctrine of Christian Discovery*

Contents

I dedicate this book to the First People of California.
May they continue to grow and prosper.

Foreword, by Valentin Lopez

As a Franciscan priest, Mark Day learned the history of California's missions from the friar's perspective. That history taught that the Indians came to the missions voluntarily to find a better life. It taught that the Indians came to learn agriculture and to find God. These lies were an intentional cover-up of the true history of California's Catholic missions, which included slavery, rape, the loss of Indigenous spirituality and knowledge, and, most tragically, the loss of humanity.

Once Day took it upon himself to learn the truth, he quickly realized the horrendous impact that these lies have caused. Since then he has worked tirelessly with the tribes to help Indigenous people heal, and he has urged the Catholic Church to recognize its role in the destruction of Indigenous people throughout the world. Mark Day recognizes his obligation to tell the truth, and he does so side by side with the Native tribes of California.

—Valentin Lopez, Chairman, Amah Mutsun
tribal band of Central California

The Formation of a Friar

"Very Reverend Father, I ask you for the love of God to admit me to the Seraphic Order of St. Francis, to do penance, to amend my life, and to serve God until death."

Those are the words my fellow novices and I recited upon our investiture to the Franciscan Order in the summer of 1960. The ceremony took place at Mission San Miguel, near the dusty town of Paso Robles in Central California.

It was dark inside the mission church. A large painting of St. Michael the Archangel loomed above the altar. Our families and friends looked on and later took photos of us in our new habits. A friar would later cut our hair in the form of a corona (crown).

Seven years earlier, I began my Franciscan formation at St. Anthony's Seminary high school, nestled in the foothills of Santa Barbara—later to become a high-end resort town. I was 13 years old, and I remember my mother crying when she left me off at the Oakland train station.

In those days, minor seminaries were commonplace. They have since been abolished, after modern psychology deemed them harmful to the psychosexual development of young men.

I was left relatively unscathed by the experience, but it has caused some tensions in my marriage. Other classmates fared quite worse. *National Catholic Reporter* revealed that in the 1960s, eleven friars sexually abused twenty-one seminarians. A full report on this is found at bishopaccountability.org, an independent watchdog based in Boston.

Moreover, two of my sister's nieces (between ages 3 and 7) were sexually abused by a Franciscan friar at Mission Santa Barbara. The cases went to trial and the girls prevailed. But the friar never faced jail time because the statute of limitations had run out. Sexual abuse of minors is the gift that keeps on giving.

Amadeo Rea, a classmate, has published a short book, *Notes from a Country Boy: A Life Outside the Lines*, about this. "We were psychological eunuchs," he wrote. "Our puberty was delayed until our late teens and beyond. They kept us in a hot-house environment. Our mail was censored and visits from families restricted."

On the positive side, the friars' strict discipline—the silence periods, punishments for cheating in study hall or cutting up at night in the dormitory—was very good for me. We were, after all, typical teenagers.

SAN LUIS REY

In 1957, my classmates and I transferred to Mission San Luis Rey, where we spent two years as laymen before our novitiate year at Mission San Miguel. We found philosophy, mostly medieval scholasticism, quite boring. But we benefited from the liberal arts courses.

I regret we never studied anthropology. We could have learned about the Natives, whose slave labor built California's missions. To us they were only bit players in this drama. When I questioned this years later, one of my classmates said, "The friars are just not interested in this, Mark."

A new generation of Indigenous scholars did not agree. They assembled a wide body of research which contradicts the settler-colonial narrative promoted by Pope Francis and the Vatican. In addition to reading the works of these scholars, I benefited by attending two years of workshops with scholars in the Critical Mission Studies program, sponsored by the University of California.

SANTA BARBARA, 1962

We felt enthusiastic about Pope John XXIII and his attempts to bring the church up to date with the modern world. Our faculty at Mission Santa Barbara was in tune with fresh currents of thought from European theologians, unlike other seminaries that were hidebound by conservative faculties.

Seven of us were ordained priests in December, 1965. We studied pastoral theology in Stockton, California, where we became involved in parish work and teaching in a local Catholic high school.

My superior was Father Alan McCoy, a social liberal who was friends with Dorothy Day of the Catholic Worker Movement. He became minister provincial and approved my transfer to Delano, California, where I worked with Cesar Chavez and the United Farm Workers union as an organizer.

Bishop Timothy Manning eventually sent word that I was to leave Delano. Chavez put his foot down, sending several striking farmworker women to Manning's office to hold a sit-in on my behalf. Threatened by the possibility of negative press coverage, Manning relented. I stayed in Delano for nearly five years. It was one of the richest experiences of my life.

I left Delano in 1970 and worked as a parish priest in Los Angeles, where I studied for a master's degree in journalism at the University of Southern California. This enabled me to get hired at Southwest College and later at West Los Angeles Community College.

I received a dispensation from the priesthood from Pope Paul VI in 1975. Years later, I worked five years as a freelance reporter in Peru, where I covered the insurgency war with the Shining Path rebels. My time there helped me understand the checkered history of the friars in Latin America and California.

This book is an attempt to make sense of the Franciscan colonization of California. I hope it sheds some light on this unfortunate chapter of history.

Preface

The colonization of California began formally in 1769 with the arrival of the Portola expedition in what is now San Diego, California. It is a story of a clash of civilizations, of suffering and death, of assimilation and resistance that continues to this day.

Today, California is home to the largest population of Native Americans in America. The richness of these cultures is on display every three years when Mission San Luis Rey hosts a pow wow with tribes from every corner of the United States (see chapter 11).

DECOLONIZATION

The traditional settler-colonial narrative is deeply entrenched in California's popular culture. Countless businesses are named after the missions, from credit unions to linen supply companies to restaurants and hotels.

The twenty-one California missions are now parish churches and tourist attractions, silent witnesses to a past that few people really understand. Controversies over the missions and the treatment of the Indians have been seething for decades, but they took center stage in 2015 when Pope Francis canonized Fray Junípero Serra at an elaborate ceremony in Washington, DC.

Tribal leaders denounced the event, pointing out the high death rates at the missions and the destruction of Indigenous culture. They contend that the true story of the missions has been whitewashed. That truth has been erased and the record needs to corrected.

Even though most colonies conquered by European powers have gained their independence, laws and customs have not changed, nor has prejudice and discrimination against Natives. True decolonization is a personal process that requires self-examination. We need to interrogate our own assumptions about how our nation was colonized, and what our own ancestors went through when they arrived on our shores.

My Irish paternal grandfather was a cable car operator in San Francisco. He was pro-union, a trait I inherited from my father, who supported the rights of working class people. My mother's father came from Bavaria and settled first in Wisconsin, then ultimately in Hayward, California. In those days, Germans were better off compared to the Irish, who arrived on rickety sailboats with barely the shirts on their backs and faced discrimination and violence from Protestant mobs.

Understanding what my ancestors went through and studying the history of nativism has helped me relate to the plight of Native Americans and all people who come to our shores seeking a better life.

THE DOCENTS

Docents who give tours at the missions refrain from telling tourists how the Indians resisted colonization, and how they actually fought pitched battles with Spanish soldiers at several missions. Instead, the docents paint a picture of peace and serenity, one of docile Natives and compassionate padres. For the most part, the contributions of the Natives have been erased and replaced by fantasies and disinformation.

I remember a conversation with Father Francis Guest, my church history professor at Mission Santa Barbara. When I asked him to explain the controversy between the friars and dissident Indigenous leaders, he said, "If you speak to the friars you will get one story, and another from the Indians." In his book *Hispanic California Revisited*, he explains, unconvincingly, how the Indians accepted corporal punishment for minor infractions for their moral failings. "It drew them closer to the sufferings of Christ," he wrote.

As students, we were asked to give tours of Missions San Luis Rey, San Miguel, and Santa Barbara. We simply parroted the traditional narrative that the Natives welcomed the friars and worked harmoniously with them in a spirit of brotherly love to build the missions. In short, we were brainwashed. We should have known better.

I discovered that the missions were not mythical Edens where the friars and Indians lived harmoniously. The Natives lived, suffered, and died in slave-like conditions. Diseases were rampant and mortality rates chilling. At most missions, the friars buried more Indians than they baptized. Native babies born there seldom lived for more than five years.

In recent years, I have taken tours of several missions. Little has changed. For the most part, docents are unprepared and unfamiliar with recent scholarship. As a result, they have erased the true story of the California missions and replaced it with fantasy narratives and disinformation.

An elderly docent at Mission Santa Barbara said that during the mission period, no Spanish soldier ever fired a shot at the Indians. When I interrupted him and said that there were pitched battles between soldiers and Indians at several missions, he responded that he was unaware of that. A German woman thanked me for my comments.

Years ago, when I attempted to organize a focus group of friars to discuss Fray Serra and the missions, my classmate Ignatius de Groot told me sternly, "Mark, the friars are not interested in this." I found that hard to believe, but I accepted Iggy's opinion. The best response I got was from a classmate I had known since my grammar school days in Oakland, California. He told me not to quote him, but said he was reticent to criticize Pope Francis. "The fact is, Mark, we love him."

I attempted to reach out to other friars, but most did not respond. I am fairly certain that the word was passed down from the provincial superior that the friars should not speak to me. That included two nationally known Franciscans.

I am still very much a Catholic. I was baptized in 1940. The church is my home, though I struggle with many of its teachings. I agree with James Joyce, who once said of Catholics, "Here comes everyone."

Preface

I cherish my years in the Franciscan Order. As a kid growing up in Oakland, I remember the friars coming to our house for gatherings. They were lovely men, dressed in their habits with the three knots symbolizing poverty, chastity, and obedience. The cowls and tunics they wore were patterned after a beggar's outfit Francis himself chose as the uniform of his followers. Centuries have passed, but the idealism has remained.

I wanted to be like these men. I don't regret following in the footsteps of the poor man of Assisi.

Introduction: With the Best of Intentions

How does one analyze the historical impact and importance of the California missions? There are a myriad of books, studies, and other publications on the topic, too much for the average reader to digest.

The main protagonists in this drama were Spanish governors and the Spanish military, the Franciscan friars, and the Native Californians, who inhabited villages along the California coastline and were lured into the missions with the promise of eternal salvation.

The California missions had two eras: first was the mission period, from the founding of Mission San Diego (1769) until the last mission was secularized in 1834 and the friars returned to Spain and Mexico. The second era began in the 1880s, when hucksters and promoters helped rebuild the missions from ruins and marketed them as tourist attractions.

Today, the missions serve as spiritual centers, parishes, retreat centers, and museums. But during the mission period they were more akin to crude labor camps and Southern cotton plantations. Once the Indians were baptized, they were not permitted to leave.

So again, how can one analyze the complex legacy of the missions? What have emerged are two approaches. One is the settler-colonial narrative, which glorifies the missions as idyllic places where friars and Indians lived in harmony, and which laid the basis for the future state of California. The other approach is that of listening to the Natives themselves, who have occupied California since time immemorial. Their voices and struggles are seldom discussed, and their story largely erased.

And how does one separate the truth from the myths and disinformation often spread at the missions themselves by the docents? The purpose of this book is to provide a fact-based narrative that relies on recent research on the missions and that honors the lives and legacies of the Indigenous population that has survived after 250 years of oppression. The long-term effects of colonization remain with us today in terms of inter-generational trauma, domestic abuse, alcoholism, and other illnesses.

Chapter one describes the arrival of the Portola expedition to San Diego in 1769 and the beginnings of Native resistance to the Spanish soldiers, which would endure during the mission period and beyond.

Chapter two discusses the California Native Americans' ancestors, a prime focus for all Indigenous peoples.

Chapter three explains the Doctrine of Discovery. A product of medieval popes, this doctrine stipulated that the Natives were heathens, literally nobodies, whose land could be taken over by Spain and Portugal. If the Natives resisted, they would be dealt with severely.

Chapter four explains who the Franciscan missionaries were and discusses their somewhat checkered history. It explores their internal struggles over the vow of poverty, their signature accomplishments as poor followers of Christ, and the role they played on both sides of the Holy Inquisition.

Chapters five and six tell the story of Fray Junípero Serra, founder of nine missions. Serra became an inquisitor after arriving in Mexico. He was truly a man of the Middle Ages, who fought against the principles of the Enlightenment, which at the time were influencing many in the Spanish government.

Subsequent chapters deal with who tells the story of the missions: the hagiographers, who focus on Serra and the friars, or the social scientists, who tell a more objective story of the missions based mostly on documents written by the friars themselves.

Other chapters deal with the current crisis of the Indigenous boarding schools in Canada and the US, a sign that the aftermath of colonization is ongoing, with new demands being made for reconciliation and reckoning. And finally, the book offers a chapter on the allies, those who join forces with Native Californians to work for reconciliation and reckoning in the uncharted waters of the future.

I leave the final judgment to those who read this book. I would love to hear what you think.

CHAPTER 1

~~~

How It All Began

On July 16, 1769, Fray Junípero Serra, flanked by a crude wooden cross and the flag of Spain, stood on the side of a hill overlooking San Diego Bay and celebrated a High Mass, Spain's first official act in the colonization of Alta California. With Serra that day was Gaspar de Portola, leader of the expedition that had set out from Loreto, in Baja California to the south, along with colonists and a handful of friars and soldiers. Nearby, a small group of Kumeyaay Indians eyed the newcomers suspiciously.

The journey north involved three ships and two overland expeditions, originating from San Blas, Nayarit, and Baja California. Spain chose the Franciscans to lead the expedition. The friars had taken over the Baja missions after the Spanish crown expelled the Jesuits from the peninsula in 1767. (Historians note that European monarchies at the time were attempting to secularize political power and saw the Jesuits as too autonomous from them. The Jesuits were reinstated in 1814.)

As the Portola expedition had trekked northward along the Baja Peninsula, the Kumeyaay reacted with curiosity, bewilderment, and eventual hostility. They knew about earlier Spanish explorations and did not trust the interlopers.

The Kumeyaay culture is at least 9,000 years old. Their primary foods were acorns, shellfish, fish, and small game. They used fire to manage their ecosystem and resources, such as berries and oak groves. Their spiritual leaders had their own medical practices and a familiarity with psychology, biology, and handling land and water resources.

The arrival of the Spanish in what is now San Diego created challenges for the Kumeyaay natives. Angered over the invasion of their land and the destruction of their plants by Spanish livestock, and furious that soldiers were raping their women, the Kumeyaay rebelled.

On the night of November 4, 1775, a force of 700 warriors from fifteen villages set fire to Mission San Diego de Alcala, killing its pastor, Father Jayme, along with a blacksmith and a carpenter. The destruction of Mission San Diego was a major, but not fatal, setback for the Franciscans.

Captain Fernando Rivera y Moncada of the San Diego presidio considered the attackers insurrectionists against the Spanish crown and wanted them executed. But Serra and the friars called for clemency, worried that executions would derail the future of the mission system. Thirteen prisoners remained in the presidio jail for a year. A few were exiled to Loreto. Although the friars, with their medieval mentality, considered the Kumeyaay rebellion the work of the Devil, others saw it as a rational response to the atrocities the Indians faced from the Spaniards.

"The revolt was not just a military action or a spiritual quest," observed anthropologist Richard Carrico in a paper he wrote for the University of California Mission Studies Program. "The sacking was a calculated reaction to increased rapes, conversions, thefts, transmittal of diseases, and fear of forced imprisonment."

"They never conquered us," said Stanley Rodriguez, a member of the Kumeyaay Santa Isabel Iipay Nation, during a phone interview in 2024. "Several skirmishes happened along the path of the expedition. They did not want the Spaniards in their territory. Serra was more concerned about the success of the mission than anything else."

Jose Gomez, current archbishop of Los Angeles, points to Serra's intervention on behalf of the prisoners as an example of his personal sanctity. He also states that Serra traveled to Mexico City on foot to present an Indian bill of rights to Viceroy Antonio Bucareli. However, there is no evidence this journey ever occurred. The erroneous idea of a bill of rights originated from Franciscan Father Noel Moholy (1916–1998), a promoter of Serra's canonization, and the Reverend Francis Weber, archivist for the Archdiocese of Los Angeles.

Nevertheless, Serra did achieve his purpose. The viceroy granted the Franciscans complete control over the education and training of the mission population. This would prove disastrous.

Gomez and other bishops have falsely compared Serra to Fray Bartolomé de Las Casas (1484–1560), a former slave owner who became a Dominican priest and returned to Spain to lobby on behalf of Indigenous rights. Bartolomé's depiction of Spanish atrocities in his book *A Short Account of the Destruction of the Indies* has become a classic in Latin American literature.

Serra, on the other hand, did not lobby for Indigenous rights. On the contrary, he advocated for the friars to have what would effectively be parental control over the Natives, as well as the authority to administer corporal punishment for those who engaged in thievery, adultery, or other minor crimes.

The Franciscans did not come to empower or liberate the Indians but to save their souls and exploit their labor as second-class Spanish citizens. Serra and his successor, Fray Fermin de Lasuén, also lobbied against proposed Spanish legislation to hand over control of the missions to the Indians after a period of ten years. The friars manipulated the vote, thus condemning California Indians to a future of powerlessness and poverty for the next 200 years.

Thus began the mission period (1769–1834) on the side of a hill in what is now Old Town San Diego. Afterward, the Portola expedition would continue north to San Francisco Bay, paving the way for the construction of the next twenty California missions.

After San Diego, Serra founded Mission San Carlos, near Monterey. It became the administrative center of the missions and Serra's headquarters. It was also an integral part of the colonization effort, since it anchored 440 miles of coastline from San Diego to San Francisco Bay, claiming it as Spanish territory.

For the next several years, Serra would have serious conflicts with Spanish California's military governors over the issue of corporal punishment. The governors were swayed by eighteenth century Enlightenment thinking that promoted respect for human rights and frowned upon the whippings Serra administered to the Indians. But Serra never budged on this, and the practice of corporal punishment lasted throughout the mission period.

When the missions were secularized in 1834, the Spanish friars returned to Mexico and Spain. The Natives, denied Spain's promise to govern themselves, continued to be deprived of their rights. Their fate had been determined centuries earlier by papal bulls declaring them heathens, and thus not entitled to the lands they had inhabited since time immemorial. This is the subject of the next chapter.

CHAPTER 2

Honoring the Ancestors

The pain inflicted on Native Californians by the mission era lingers on today, prompting many to work hard to keep the memories of their ancestors alive within the hearts of their people.

Caroline Ward, of the Fernandeño Tataviam band of mission Indians, thought about her ancestors when she heard Pope Francis was about to canonize Fray Serra, founder of nine California missions. Her tribal ancestors play a significant role in her life and are a crucial part of her attachments to her people's land, culture, and Indigenous spirituality. Others in her band feel the same way.

Ward and I had several long conversations about her pilgrimage to the missions. Several years ago, Ward attended a workshop with Elias Castillo, whose book, *A Cross of Thorns: The Enslavement of California's Indians by the Spanish Missions*, challenges the romantic myths of saintly friars and docile Indians. His book unflinchingly documents how mass incarcerations, cruel punishments, forced labor, and disease caused the deaths of more than 75,000 Natives from 1769 to 1834.

"I felt I had to do something about the canonization," she said. So as a first step, she walked the fifteen miles from the present-day Six Flags Magic Mountain theme park to the San Fernando Mission, where her tribe was based. Ward saw the Six Flags walk as the beginning of her journey.

After this initial walk, Ward decided to trek to all the missions, from the San Francisco Bay Area missions that had subjected the Miwok people south to Mission San Diego, which

Caroline Ward. *Public domain.*

housed the Kumeyaay. Kagen, her son, joined her on this trek. They reached out to friends and quickly developed a support network to spread the message. Hundreds of Natives joined her along the way, from Sonoma to San Diego. The walk attracted media attention and raised consciousness among the tribes and the general public about Serra's impending canonization.

The pilgrimage began at Mission San Francisco Solano on September 7, 2015, and ended on November 7 at Mission San Diego. Their feet would be blistered at first, but they gradually made their way from mission to mission. At each mission, they would greet Indigenous leaders, pray, sing, and share stories about their ancestors. They camped out frequently, occasionally spent nights at motels, and frequently accepted lodging from friends and strangers.

MISSIONS SAN FRANCISCO SOLANO AND SAN RAFAEL

At Mission San Francisco Solano, they read aloud the names of 938 baptized Indians of the Ohlone and Coastal Miwok tribes. Tragically, Native children living at the missions often did not live past age seven. Demoralized by this, Fray Mariano Payeras wrote: "Even the most pious will answer, 'The missionary priest baptized them, administered the sacraments and buried them.'"

Yet Payeras and other friars blamed the Natives for living in filthy and crowded dormitories, for their poor health, and for their "bad habits of barbarism and heathenism." (For further context, see Dr. Jonathan Cordero's statements in chapters five and eight.)

When Caroline and Kagen arrived at Mission San Rafael the next day, they asked where the Indians were buried. "Over there, under the parking lot," said a church employee. This response was typical.

MISSIONS DOLORES, SAN JOSE, AND SAN CARLOS (CARMEL)

At Mission Dolores, they discovered that Indigenous remains were scattered beneath the streets and homes of the Mission District.

At Mission San Jose, they met with a parish priest and with Ohlone matriarch Corina Gould. Gould chided the priest for supporting the Serra canonization. "If Serra were a saint, he would have stopped the destruction and devastation," she said. "I ask you to stand taller than Serra."

Their visit to Mission San Carlos (Carmel-by-the-Sea) coincided with the Serra canonization ceremony being broadcasted from Washington, DC, on a live television feed. Louise Miranda, chairwoman of the Ohlone Costanoan Esselen nation, led a prayer circle. "I'm glad you have come to show respect for our ancestors," she said. "They know we will never forget them."

Nearby stood Laughing Coyote (Mono tribe). "It's not just about Serra," he said. "The Catholic Church as an institution was complicit in the murder, kidnapping, torture, and destruction of a whole race of people. These are not sins. They are criminal acts."

MISSIONS SANTA CRUZ, SAN MIGUEL, AND SAN JUAN CAPISTRANO

At Mission Santa Cruz, volunteer Cat Wilder insisted that the land be restored to local tribes. He asked, "What do the Ohlone own in Santa Cruz County today? Nothing! There is ongoing genocide taking place right now."

At Mission San Miguel, Caroline and Kagen learned that pastor Fray Antonio Horra had written a letter to the viceroy, accusing the friars of severely whipping and shackling the Natives without giving them a drop of water. In response, his superior, Fray Fermin de Lasuén, insisted that Natives were a "savage population who deserved strong punishments." Horra was declared insane and deported to Mexico City.

Caroline and Kagen were welcomed at Mission San Juan Capistrano on November 1 by Acjachemen elders and friends. Spiritual leader Adelia Sandoval led a procession of fifty elders. They stood beside an ancient wall containing stones and seashells placed there 200 years ago. "When we touch them, we touch the ancestors," she said.

The mission is set among trendy restaurants and tourist shops. It features Christmas lights, concerts, candlelight dinners, a mariachi festival, and "music under the stars." This has prompted some critics to call San Juan Capistrano "the Disneyland of all the missions." There is no evidence that the Natives benefit financially from the tourist dollars.

MISSIONS SAN LUIS REY AND SAN DIEGO

Caroline and Kagen joined a group benefit of some twenty-five supporters on a cold, drizzly evening on the steps of the San Luis Rey mission church. It was dark, except for an occasional lightning flash. Most participants were Luiseño (Payaomkawhum) Natives. Chairman Mel Vernon welcomed the visitors to their territory.

"My great-grandparents were slaves here at the mission," said Max Moran, a stocky man in his sixties. "It breaks my heart that all this is hidden. People think the missions did so much, but to us it was just destruction. It makes me angry."

Luiseño council member Marlene Fosselman said it was important to remember that the missions were only a small part of Luiseño history. She added, gesturing toward the church, "If it were not for our people, what would they have had?"

"Iipai-Kumeyaay dancers from both sides of the border were there," said tribal chairman Stanley Rodriguez of the Santa Ysabel (Kumeyaay nation) reservation. "Our people went to war. But we still have our language. We still have our songs. We are still Native people. We are still resisting. We have not been defeated."

Laughing Coyote from the Mono tribe gifted those present with eagle feathers from the Sierras. "With the Serra canonization, I was waiting for someone to lead the way," he said. "I cannot begin to express my gratitude to Caroline and Kagen."

CHAPTER 3

~~~

The Blueprint for Conquest (Doctrine of Discovery)

Pope Nicolas wasn't messing around when he issued the papal bull *Romanus Pontifex* ("the Roman Pontiff") to King Alfonso of Portugal in 1452. The decree declared war against all non-Christians in the world, directing that "Saracens, pagans and other enemies of Christ be captured, subdued, put into perpetual slavery and deprived of their possessions and property." It was part of the Doctrine of Christian Discovery, which justified European colonial expansion into non-Christian lands. And despite its draconian and violent language, the Vatican has never rescinded it.

The Doctrine of Discovery has been cropping up lately in both the secular and religious presses. It was even featured in a lengthy CBS news report featuring leading Protestant theologian Jim Wallis of *Sojourners* magazine. Steven Newcomb (Shawnee/Lenape), author of *Pagans in the Promised Land:*

Decoding the Doctrine of Christian Discovery, has been researching the topic for thirty years. What astounds him is the Vatican's lack of familiarity with the doctrine. "One archbishop told me, 'To be honest, I confess I've never read it,'" Newcomb told me when I interviewed him. Several attempts to petition the Vatican for abrogating the doctrine have gone unanswered.

Newcomb argues that the papal bulls of 1451 (Pope Nicolas V) and 1493 (Pope Alexander VI) justified Spain's and Portugal's "grim acts of genocide and conquest" committed by Christopher Columbus, Juan Pizarro in Peru, Diego de Almagro in Chile, and Hernan de Cortez in Mexico. Four hundred years later, Supreme Court justice John Marshall extended the doctrine to the United States, ruling in 1835 that Natives could not own land, only occupy it.

Newcomb notes that the Doctrine of Discovery raised its ugly head with the colonization of the Americas, then later with broken treaties, poverty-stricken reservations, and high mortality rates at Indigenous boarding schools. It is active even today, with ongoing assaults against Native peoples already suffering from intergenerational trauma, sickness, and political powerlessness.

In my experience, both the Franciscans and the Catholic bishops have failed to address the Doctrine of Discovery, relying on hagiographical writings to praise Serra and the Franciscan missionaries. They have ignored the findings of historians and other social scholars. One friar asked how me how he could accept any blame. "I wasn't there," he said. "How can you blame me for this?"

An early report on the destructive impact of the Doctrine of Discovery was made by the aforementioned Bartolomé de Las Casas. Numerous rebellions against the Spaniards occurred during the colonial period. But no one described the atrocities better than de Las Casas, a former landowner who possessed slaves. After witnessing the barbarism of the Spanish soldiers, he had a change of heart. He became a priest and recorded his eyewitness experiences in his previously mentioned book, *A Short Account of the Destruction of the Indies*, published in 1552. "The soldiers with their spears and lances entered into the villages, sparing neither children nor old men and women," he wrote. "They ripped open their bellies and cut them to pieces. They took little ones by their heels and crushed their heads against cliffs. Others they threw into the rivers. They put everyone they met to the edge of the sword."

Pope Francis knew this when he visited Bolivia in 2015, offering a powerful mea culpa for the "offenses and crimes of the conquest." Standing next to him was leftist President Evo Morales, son of Aymara-speaking subsistence farmers.

Bolivia's Potosi silver mines were a graveyard for eight million Indians over a period of three centuries, according to historian Eduardo Galeano. In his seminal work, *Open Veins in Latin America: Five Centuries of the Pillage of a Continent*, Galeano wrote that women and children were torn from their agricultural communities and driven to El Cerro Rico Mountain. "Of every ten who went up into the freezing wilderness," he wrote, "seven never returned. Many women returned as widows and countless children were orphaned."

There is a deep irony about this because Francis made his apology just two months before traveling to Washington, DC, to canonize Fray Serra, the controversial founder of nine California missions. Francis probably did not anticipate the strong backlash to his announcement. For most California Indians, it was a slap in the face, a papal blunder, and a setback for relations between the tribes, the Catholic Church, and the Franciscan Order.

THE TRAGEDY OF THE BOARDING SCHOOLS

The ramifications of the Doctrine of Discovery remain. Its long-term effects continue. Both Canada and the United States are currently facing unprecedented scandals of sexual abuse and unsolved deaths at Indian boarding and residential schools.

The Carlisle Indian Industrial School opened in 1879 in Carlisle, Pennsylvania. The motto of Lt. Col. Richard Henry Pratt, its founder, was "Kill the Indian, save the man." In the aftermath of the Indian wars, the US military took charge of Indian education. Soldiers were designated, just as the Spanish friars were many years earlier, to take the place of Native parents. When the students arrived, their hair was cut, their names were changed, their tribal clothing was prohibited, and they were told to stop speaking their native languages. To enforce conformity and obedience, children were traumatized by corporal punishment and solitary confinement and stripped of their religious beliefs, culture, and heritage. Hundreds died from white men's diseases.

According to NPR.org, the government operated 400 such Indian boarding schools on reservations, and religious groups throughout the country started their own boarding schools.[1] (It wasn't until 1978, with the passage of the Indian Child Welfare Act, that Native American parents had the legal right to deny their children's placement in off-reservation schools.) In recent years, hundreds of graves at former boarding schools have been uncovered in the United States and Canada. Preston McBride of the University of Southern California believes there could be as many as 40,000 such graves across the United States. So far, 1,300 bodies have been discovered in the US. A formal investigation is just beginning.[2] Senator Elizabeth Warren (D-Mass) and former Interior Department Secretary Deb Haaland introduced legislation seeking healing for those who have suffered trauma at the schools.

In response to a boarding school investigation from the US Department of the Interior, the United States Conference of Catholic Bishops has begun dialogues with tribal leaders on boarding school accountability. Archbishop Paul S. Coakley of Oklahoma City wrote to his fellow bishops that conditions at the schools were "very bad, if not disastrous." He lamented the forced assimilation of children, cruelly separated from their parents and denied access to their languages and cultural identity. "In addition to allegations of abuse and neglect, children ran away. Their families to this day do not know what

1. https://www.npr.org/2024/07/30/nx-s1-5051912/interior-dept-report-indian-boarding-schools
2. https://www.npr.org/sections/codeswitch/2021/08/28/1031398120/native-boarding-schools-repatriation-remains-carlisle

happened to their loved ones." Coakley is urging the bishops to cooperate with the government "as a meaningful step toward healing."

BOARDING SCHOOLS IN CANADA

Children in Canada were forced into state-funded Christian schools from the nineteenth century until the 1970s, isolating them from their families and tribes. Almost three quarters of the residential schools were run by Catholic missionaries. Following the church's colonial policy, Indigenous children were ripped from their families, traditions, and culture.

Pope Francis issued an apology to Native Canadians on April 1, 2022, after listening to their stories at the Vatican. "I want to tell you I am greatly pained," said the Pope, meeting at the Vatican with three separate Native groups. "And I unite myself with the Canadian bishops in apologizing."

"The pope's words today were historic, and I appreciate them deeply," said Cassidy Caron, president of the Metis National Council. "I look forward to his visit to Canada."

The Canadian government admits that most children in Canadian residential schools have suffered sexual abuse, and thus far the deaths of more than 4,100 Indigenous children have been reported.[3] There are no coping mechanisms to deal with the pain of children separated from their parents. A CBS broadcast by Anderson Cooper in 2023 included poignant

---

3. https://www.cbc.ca/news/indigenous/permanent-peoples-tribunal-residential-schools-1.7362471

interviews with victims, who told harrowing stories about being abused and separated.[4]

Canada established its own Truth and Reconciliation Commission in 2007. It provided $72 million to support its work and relied on the testimony of 6,500 witnesses. The TRC adopted the United Nations Declaration of Rights of Indigenous people, establishing a universal framework of minimum standards for the survival, dignity, and well-being of the Indigenous peoples of the world.

THE SITUATION IN CALIFORNIA

I have had many discussions with Native Californians who have told me that their family members had suffered abuse at Indian boarding schools in California. It turned them away from the Catholic Church.

"These crimes committed against California Native children while forced and kidnapped to attend these California Native Boarding Schools must be acknowledged by the Christian Churches and their institutions that ran them and [they must be] held accountable for the crimes they committed against our children from 1850 to the 1960s. California must reckon with our dark history of violence, discrimination, and exploitation sanctioned by the state government throughout its history."

This was a 2021 statement from the California chapter of the United Warrior Society, given in reaction to Governor Gavin Newsom's apology and the Truth and Healing Council

4. https://www.cbsnews.com/news/canada-residential-schools-un-marked-graves-indigenous-children-60-minutes-transcript-2023-05-28

he established to counter the conventional fantasy narrative about Native Americans and the missions.

Newsom said, "We can never undo the wrongs inflicted on the peoples who have lived on his land since time immemorial. But we can work together to build bridges, tell the truth, and begin to heal deep wounds."

Just before Newsom took office in 2018, former Governor Jerry Brown issued a proclamation admitting the past failings of the state toward its Indigenous population. Brown criticized Spain and Mexico, "who through disease and enslavement cut the Indigenous population by more than a half from 1769 to 1834."

The 1849 Gold Rush brought more violence and disease. In 1851, Governor Peter Burnett authorized killing Indians for bounty in a "war of extermination until the Indian race becomes extinct." By 1900, California's Indigenous population had been reduced by 80 percent. But the Native population rebounded, and California today is home to the largest population of Native Americans in the fifty states. Governor Brown observed, "If Governor Burnett could not envision a future California that included Native Americans, it is just as impossible for us today to envision one without them."

Perhaps as a part of this healing, the Franciscans and the California bishops should take an active role in dialoguing with the state's First Peoples. They will learn, as others have, that oppressors, just like the oppressed, need healing too.

THE REPUDIATION OF THE DOCTRINE OF CHRISTIAN DISCOVERY

For decades, it was hoped that the Vatican would put the Doctrine of Christian Discovery to rest by rescinding it, as most mainline Protestant churches and the Unitarian Universalist Association had urged for many years. Indigenous peoples were never "discovered," and their resilience in the face of 500 years of oppression is an example for us all.

The Vatican finally repudiated the Doctrine of Discovery in April 2023, but its long-term effects are still apparent, the boarding school tragedies in Canada and the United States being among the most notable examples.

But significant attempts at healing have occurred. Some religious orders owned slaves. In 1838, the Jesuits of what is now Georgetown University sold 272 slaves for $115,000 to pay their real estate debts. In 2021, the Jesuits agreed to pay $100 million in reparations, mostly to 5,000 descendants of the slaves.

Additionally, Virginia Theological Seminary paid out $1.7 million in reparations,[5] and Princeton Theological Seminary provided $27 million in scholarships to African American students in Louisiana.[6]

The Sacred Heart of Jesus's sisters decided to create a scholarship fund for the descendants of slaves they owned in Louisiana and Missouri. The sisters utilized the metaphor of

5. https://www.nytimes.com/2021/05/31/us/reparations-virginia-theological-seminary.html
6. https://www.nytimes.com/2019/10/21/nyregion/princeton-seminary-slavery-reparations.html

a broken heart reaching out for healing in their group reflections. "True repentance is transformation in thinking that leads to action," said Krisi Laughlin, a Sacred Heart Society lay associate. "We need to repent for the racism that contributed to the blind spot in our history."

"From broken to blessed, the wound stays open, the heart exposed, giving love, receiving our love," said Sacred Heart associate Molly Arthur. "Then we can live in a broken and blessed world as artisans of hope."

CHAPTER 4

~ ~ ~

Who Are the Franciscans?

I was a thirteen-year-old freshman when I took my first class in Franciscan history at St. Anthony's Seminary in Santa Barbara from Father Lionel. He was a tall, lean, gentle man, who wore horn-rimmed glasses with lenses like coke bottles.

He told us that Francis Pietro di Bernadone was the son of a wealthy cloth merchant and a carefree *bon vivant* in thirteenth-century Italy. But Francis was shocked at how new wealth had created social inequalities and dire poverty, so he organized a group of his peers to sleep in doorways with the homeless and to preach the gospel to the poor.

Francis's father, Pietro di Bernadone, did not approve of his son's new behavior. But what ruptured the relationship of father and son was that Francis sold some of his merchant father's valuable cloth to raise money to assist a local priest in paying for church repairs. Pietro beat Francis and locked him in a storage room. Petra, his mother, freed him, and the matter was referred to the local bishop for arbitration. At that point Francis renounced his inheritance, stripped himself naked, and said, "Up to now, Pietro di Bernadone, I have called you father. But from now on, I pray, 'Our father, who art in heaven.'"

That story might be apocryphal, but it set the scene for the future. Once Francis got approval from Pope Innocent III,[7] his newly founded Order of the Lesser Brothers would grow exponentially to all parts of the world. Within ten years there were 5,000 friars in the order. There would be struggles as well, especially his devotion to living a life of material deprivation, which Francis called his vow to "Lady Poverty."

As the centuries passed, the friars would divide into three branches: the Observants, who followed the Rule of St. Francis strictly; the Conventuals, who focused on building parish communities; and the Capuchins, with their emphasis on prayer and contemplation. Over the years, several other branches were to develop among both religious men and women.

Junípero Serra belonged to one of these lesser groups, a strict offshoot of the Observants called the Alcantarans. They practiced severe forms of mortifications and renounced creature comforts such as riding horseback or in carriages. Serra served tables, cleaned kitchen floors, and served meals to his brothers. Serra's supporters believed this, plus his penitential practices and personal sacrifices as a missionary, qualified him for sainthood. But opponents believed Serra's harsh policies toward the Indians were disastrous, causing widespread

---

7. Of interest, Innocent III was played flawlessly by Sir Alec Guinness in the film *Brother Sun, Sister Moon*.

sicknesses, death, and the long-term destruction of their culture. This, they say, is the man's true legacy.

COLONIZING THE AMERICAS

St. Francis died in 1226, but the Franciscan Order, as noted above, grew rapidly throughout all parts of the world. It would be radically different 266 years later (1492), when the friars were chosen by the Spanish crown to oversee the conquest and colonization of the Americas. Julia McClure, in her groundbreaking book *The Franciscan Invention of the New World*, shows how the friars' ideals were compromised when emperors and kings granted them special powers and privileges.

Fray Juan de Zumárraga was Mexico's first bishop and one of its best known inquisitors. He was known for legitimizing the apparition of the Virgin of Guadalupe, seen by an Indian named Juan Diego in 1531, and encouraging her veneration. This event greatly increased the enrollment of Indigenous Mexicans in the Catholic Church. Not all scholars believe in the apparition's historicity. And Father Stafford Pool (1930–2020), a church history professor in California, claimed that the Guadalupe devotion wasn't popularized until 1648 by a Mexican priest. Pool wrote that it originated from the *criollos* (Spaniards born in Mexico), not the Indians. Pool concluded there was no valid documentation to prove Juan Diego ever existed and that Pope John Paul II should not have canonized him. Whatever one thinks, the cult of Guadalupe unified Mexico's Indigenous population and spread to all of Latin America.

Zumárraga was a complex person. He was known as the "defender of the Indians," but he oversaw the destruction of all of the ancient Maya codices. He also executed 157 Amerindians accused of witchcraft. They were placed on a scaffold, scourged, shaved, and dressed in penitent clothing.

The friars' long-term goal was to destroy the pagan idols and temples and to replace them with a vibrant, Indigenous Christian community based on love and simplicity. But it was not so much an invitation to faith as it was an imposition by force of arms. The Franciscans accomplished this by a top-down campaign to destroy Aztec culture and replace it with Guadalupana Catholicism. To help accomplish this, a group of friars called the Twelve Apostles established schools for some 5,000 Native children, catechetical programs, and hospitals. They learned the Nahua language and taught students how to inform on their parents to monitor pagan practices. It worked because the Natives trusted the friars, with their thread-bare tunics and bare feet. They saw them sleeping on the ground and eating tortillas, their daily bread. The friars shared the Indians' poverty, unlike those who came looking for precious metals or to exploit them.

It was not until over two centuries later (1769) that the Portola expedition and Serra arrived in Alta California. With few colonists and no established towns, it was Indian labor that built the twenty-one missions along the California coast.

Unlike in Mexico, the Indigenous people of California were provided no schools or hospitals, only crude labor camps. Once Natives were baptized, they could not leave the missions.

When they escaped, they were captured and punished. This created resentment, and heavily armed soldiers were needed to protect the missionaries, a lesson learned after massacres in New Mexico and Arizona. Decades earlier, Franciscan missionaries had accompanied Juan de Onate's soldiers to New Mexico, where the soldiers attacked the Acoma pueblo in 1599, killing 800 Indians. The pueblos later revolted, murdering 400 settlers and 28 friars. And in 1781, Quechan Indians attacked two Spanish missions near Yuma, Arizona, killing 100 settlers and four friars. The Spaniards retreated, conceding victory to the Quechans.

In California, the Spanish took no chances. When the Portola expedition arrived in San Diego Bay and Spain claimed Alta California as its possession to prevent other European powers from getting a foothold in the state, small groups of Indians tried to scare off the soldiers and friars. They quickly discovered the lethal power of Spanish muskets and armor. Soon afterwards, the soldiers began raping Kumeyaay women and running their livestock on Indian land. This planted the seeds of rebellion, resulting in the destruction of Mission San Diego and the killing of its pastor, Father Luis Jaime, in 1775.

My own Franciscan journey took many twists and turns since I took that class from Father Lionel. St. Francis captured our youthful idealism, but his friars left a mixed legacy in Latin America. It is difficult to measure their successes and failures because faith and conversions are hard to quantify. One can only speculate and probe the hearts of descendants to determine where that faith is today.

But one thing that is clear is the lingering impact of the colonial and post-colonial periods. If you drive around San Diego County, you will notice several cities named after Spanish land grants: Rancho Buena Vista, Rancho Bernardo, and Rancho Penasquitos, for example. These extensive lands were divided up by Mexican officials when the Mexican government took over from the Spanish crown. The Natives were reduced to grinding poverty and the status of day laborers. The loss of land is one of the biggest tragedies of the colonization of California.

Recently, Mission San Luis Rey constructed a retirement center on its property called La Hacienda. It caters to wealthy people who enjoy the mission's beautiful setting and regard it as their personal country club. It is a far cry from the stated goal of the Franciscan Order, which was founded to serve the poor, not the rich. This is not what I signed up for when I joined the order. I am disheartened to see that no friars objected to this. The vow of poverty also implies that the friars not only renounce earthly possessions but speak out against the many forms of abuse and exploitation the Indians face on a daily basis.

CHAPTER 5

~~~

Serra, the Founding Father

Serra was born on the Spanish Mediterranean island of Majorca in 1713. At five feet, two inches in height, he compensated for his short stature by his toughness of spirit. He was attracted to the Franciscan Order, like many of us were, though friendships with local friars. He joined the Franciscan noviatiate at age 17, was ordained a priest in 1737, and later taught theology in Palma, Majorca. He volunteered for the missions in 1749, serving as novice master at the Apostolic College of San Fernando in Mexico City. Later he spent decades in the Sierra Gorda missions of Queretaro, where he was appointed an officer of the Holy Inquisition.

Serra's toughest case was that of Maria Pasquala de Nava, a non-Native Christian who was accused of witchcraft and arrested by Spanish soldiers. Serra was convinced she was guilty for casting a spell on a woman of mixed ancestry who allegedly was in league with the devil. Maria denied the charges in an interview with Serra. He found her guilty and

Father Junípero Serra. *Creative Commons license.*

she was sentenced to a flea-infested dungeon in Mexico City. There she was found mortally wounded on the ground outside her cell. A priest anointed her, and she died shortly afterward.

In his book *Junípero Serra: California's Founding Father*, historian Steven Hackel wrote that Serra was wary of Maria Pasquala because she was a woman and a widow. Her racial background also made him suspicious, since she was a "mulata." Besides, commented Hackel, Spanish men at that time "viewed all women as weak and vulnerable to temptation, especially those without husbands."

California's Catholic bishops tell us today that Serra was a "man of his time." Actually, he lived during the Enlightenment, when reason, not force, had become the source of authority. The fresh winds of tolerance, fraternity, and constitutional government were sweeping across Europe and New England, replacing kings, domination, obedience, and imperial edicts. Serra swam against these currents.

Spanish governors and officers knew this and admonished Serra to avoid excesses in punishing the Indians. They also urged Serra to follow Spanish law, which required Natives to assume governance of the missions after a period of ten years. Serra resisted and, years later, his decision caused widespread evictions of Indians when the missions were secularized (decommissioned) in 1834. California mission lands were taken over by Mexican officials and distributed to their cronies. Serra and his successor, Fermin de Lasuén, ensured that the Indians would wind up in dire poverty for generations.

Serra also followed another medieval practice: self-flagellation. This act was promoted by the church as a form of mortification in response to war, famine, and plagues. Serra often whipped himself with a chain while preaching at Mass in Mexico City. On one occasion, a man climbed to the pulpit, took the chain, and beat himself until he collapsed. He died as a consequence.

Serra died at Mission San Carlos on August 28, 1784. Despite his many unenlightened viewpoints, the Catholic Church continues promoting the colonial narrative, emphasizing Serra's holiness and his status as "the apostle of

California." Archbishops Jose Gomez of Los Angeles and Salvatore Cordileone of San Francisco have made statements that Native historians find questionable. As noted in chapter 1, Gomez says that Serra walked 4,000 miles from Mission San Carlos to Mexico City to present "an Indigenous bill of rights" to Viceroy Antonio Bucareli.

"Not true," sociologist Jonathan Cordero (Ohlone/ Chumash) of California Lutheran University wrote in his blog. "Serra did not walk from Monterey to Mexico City, nor did he author a bill of rights. Franciscan Father Noel Moholy (a

Father Junípero Serra celebrates Mass at Monterey.
Painting by Léon Trousset. *Public domain.*

postulator for Serra's canonization) concocted the bill of rights story. Nowhere is there a record of such rights for Native people. Moholy made that up." And as for Serra's supposed journey on foot, Cordero notes that "Serra took a boat to San Diego, and another to San Blas, Nayarit [in Mexico], then he traveled by mule to the capital."

Cordero writes that Serra traveled to Mexico with the sole purpose of assuming complete control over the training, education, and governance of the missions. Serra did want to protect the Indians from the abuses of the soldiers, "But the truth is that the friars controlled everything that happened at the missions. Serra wanted total control, but the governors and civil authorities wanted to give the Natives more freedoms." Serra achieved his goal, much to the long-term detriment of the Indians.

According to the California Mission Foundation (CMF), the Indigenous population in California at the time of the arrival of the Portola Expedition in 1769 was more then 300,000. The Natives suffered a catastrophically high mortality rate during the decades afterward, mainly due to factors such as overwork, poor diet, depression caused by separation of parents and children, and excessive corporal punishment for offenses such as theft and adultery.

The CMF reports that 80,000 Indians were baptized between 1769 and 1834. Life expectancy for those baptized and brought into the missions was nine years, though many died after four years. "The Franciscans knew there would be high death rates, because they read about past experiences," wrote Professor Cordero. "That's called genocide. This is intentional ignorance."

Fray Mariano Payeras, the last president of the missions, lamented the deaths. But in a letter he wrote to the viceroy in Mexico City, he defended the friars, blaming the Indians instead for their "wretched way of life": "Soon there will be no Indians left. What will they say about us?"

Cordero and other Indigenous scholars insist that the focus should not be on the character of Serra but on the system itself. In his personal blog, Cordero writes, "Our goal should be to get the Franciscans and California's bishops to tell the truth." That is the subject of the next chapter.

CHAPTER 6

~~~

Making Saint Serra

"That the spiritual fathers shall present their sons, the Indians, with blows appears to be as old as the conquest of the Americas. Two or three whippings applied to them may serve for them and the rest a warning of spiritual benefit for them all."—Saint Serra

"I humbly ask forgiveness, not only for the offenses of the Church herself, but also for crimes committed against Native peoples during the so-called conquest of America," said Pope Francis, speaking in Bolivia in July, 2015. Yet two months later, on a visit to the United States, he canonized Fray Junípero Serra, the controversial founder of the California mission system. California tribal leaders reacted swiftly. They asked how the Pope could denounce the crimes of the Spanish conquest, yet disregard the voices of the Native descendants who still suffer trauma from Serra's policies.

Pope Francis prepared for the canonization by rolling out his plans on a visit to the Pontifical North America College in Rome, where Catholic seminarians prepare themselves for leadership positions in the church as future monsignors and bishops.

Anticipating Serra's critics, historian Robert M. Senkewicz of Santa Clara University repeated a common talking point: "Nobody is perfect. Serra was a man who tried to make conditions for the Indians as humane as possible." Senkewicz and his wife, Rose Marie Beebe, were hired by the Franciscan Order to write a book about Serra to promote his canonization.[8] Others expressed similar sentiments in defense of Serra.

The canonization elicited strong opposition from Native Californians, who accuse Serra of mistreating the Indians he sought to convert to Catholicism. While his defenders call him a holy and ascetic man who loved and protected the Indians and laid the foundations for the golden state, Native leaders accuse him of authorizing corporal punishment when Indians broke rules and shirked their duties at the missions.

In a last ditch attempt to halt the proceedings, tribal leaders held a press conference on September 15, 2015, denouncing the canonization ceremony. "It was Serra who developed the mission system," said Valentin Lopez, chairman of the Amah Mutsun tribe. "Francis has opened the door to the church's dark and tragic history with Native Americans." Lopez, who grew up Catholic, wrote four letters to Pope Francis without receiving a reply. He said an online petition with 10,000 signatures was also sent to the Pope. Fifty-five other tribes also wrote to the pope without receiving any responses.

---

8. Rose Marie Beebe, Robert M. Senkewicz. *Junípero Serra: California, Indians, and the Transformation of a Missionary* (University of Oklahoma Press, 2020).

Deborah Miranda, an elder of the Ohlone-Costanoan nation, told reporters: "Serra was not the face of evil, but so many atrocities were happening and he closed his eyes. I don't think he should be rewarded for that."

Poet Suzan Shown Harjo (Cheyenne and Hodulgee Muscogee) voiced her concerns, asking the pope to rescind the Doctrine of Discovery and reverse the canonization: "These papal bulls and the Doctrine of Discovery have sanctioned land thefts and the dehumanization of Native Peoples from the fifteenth century to the present time. Father Serra embodied the Catholic Church's institutional disrespect for Native peoples' religions, sovereignty, families, languages, laws, treaties, boundaries, ways, and lives, and he should not be elevated to sainthood for his actions."

Despite the many protestations, on September 23, 2015, the Serra canonization took place outdoors in Washington, DC, at the National Shrine of the Immaculate Conception in a sunny open air Mass before an enthusiastic congregation of 23,000. A large banner of Serra hung over the altar. In the VIP section, scores of bishops and priests sat, dressed in white albs. Pope Francis's homily focused on the church's missionary theology, with only a few remarks about Serra's physical stamina and his famous motto: "Always look forward, never turn backwards."

The Pope's remark that "Serra was a protector of Native peoples during a time of colonial exploitation" may have impressed the faithful but failed to move his critics. "It was like rubbing salt in the wounds," said Caroline Ward, who made a two-month pilgrimage to the missions to respect her ancestors (see chapter 2).

Pope Francis regards Serra not only as a holy man but as an example of an immigrant who suffered enormous physical hardships. But it seems unlikely that today's immigrants would know enough about Serra to venerate him. There has never been a groundswell of support for Serra's canonization, except among the Catholic hierarchy and the Franciscan Order.

This is in contrast to Archbishop Oscar Romero, who was assassinated for denouncing the abuses and murders of the Salvadoran military. In saint-making, popular support is everything. One could say the same for Dorothy Day of the Catholic Worker Movement, another candidate for canonization. She was deeply religious, but also controversial due to her pacifism, socialism, and anti-imperialism. But even conservative Cardinal Timothy Dolan of New York supported her cause.

Some pursued sainthood for Serra while he was still alive, but the formal process started in the 1940s. It made little progress until Popes John Paul II and Francis called for Serra's canonization. The announcement by Francis surprised even the Franciscans.

In his book *Making Saints: How the Catholic Church Determines Who Becomes a Saint, Who Doesn't, and Why*, former *Newsweek* reporter Kenneth Woodward shows how the canonization process became complicated, expensive, and politicized over the centuries. Early saints were proclaimed by popular demand. Then the lawyers took over, turning it into a purely juridical process.

THE BEATIFICATION

Pope John Paul II's reforms placed the process in the hands of local bishops. But when Serra's beatification took place in 1988, Thaddeus Shubsda, the bishop of Monterey/Fresno, disregarded the complaints of Native American scholars such as Rupert and Jeannette Costo, authors of *Natives of the Golden State: The California Indians*. The Costos wrote: "The most important story to come out of California is one of horrifying genocide, first in the missions, then through the Mexican successors, and finally to the gruesome story of the Gold Rush in 1849."

Shubsda accused the Costos and Native leaders of "poor research" and rejected their contentions. I followed this discussion and was appalled by Bishop Shubsda's heavy-handed dealings with Rupert and Jeannette Costo. He disrespected them and stacked the deck against them. This was not a proud moment for the California bishops.

Shubsda instead handpicked nine scholars who agreed with him. These scholars minimized the mortality rate at the missions and rejected any accusations of cruelty against Fray Serra.

One such scholar, Father Francis Guest, my former church history professor, wrote: "Such charges have no foundation. There was a custom whereby the missionaries, as legal guardians, imposed corporal punishment on the badly behaved, a practice that had been followed in the missions of Spanish America for two centuries." Others reacted by comparing the missions to concentration camps. "That's absurd," wrote history professor Doyce Nunis. "Those camps were meant to destroy. The missions were set up to save."

The Vatican agreed with Shubsda and approved the beatification. The outcry was so great that the ceremony was moved from California and took place at the Vatican

Valentin Lopez, chairman of the Amah Mutsun tribe. *Courtesy Valentin Lopez.*

on September 25, 1988. Washington also proved a safer venue for the canonization, given the heated protests from tribal leaders and scholars. Better, they thought, to have the ceremony 3,000 miles to the east rather than hold it in the "belly of the beast."

According to Catholic theology, a papal canonization is final and irrevocable. It means that Saint Junípero Serra is in heaven. Some theologians believe that the Pope's word is infallible, though others disagree. In any case, Catholics must accept his decision. You cannot undo a canonization. But this does not mean that the controversy is settled. Protests will continue. Statues of the colonizers and mission bells will continue tumbling down, and the debates will go on.

CHAPTER 7

~~~

Who Gets to Tell the Story?

The story of Fray Serra and the twenty-one California missions has deep roots. It was told initially by Serra's fellow friars, such as fellow Majorcan Fray Francisco Palou, and later by friar historians such as Franciscan Father Zephyryn Engelhardt, Maynard Geiger, and more recently by Francis Guest, my church history professor at the Franciscan School of Theology in Santa Barbara.

The genre was hagiography, otherwise known as the lives of the saints. There was never any thought that the First People had any agency or anything important to offer. They were considered heathens in need of salvation. The friars were concerned about saving their souls, not so much their bodies.

Nevertheless, the friars were meticulous record keepers, faithfully documenting all events and policies at the missions. Their records included sicknesses, diseases, deaths, and punishments that befell the Indians at the missions, even long after they were decommissioned and secularized in 1834. The bottom line is that the friars transformed the Natives into second-class Spanish citizens who provided cheap labor to build and maintain the missions.

Francisco Palou was a former philosophy student of Serra. He followed him to Mexico and later to California. His book *Relación Histórica de la Vida del Venerable Padre Fray Junípero Serra* went through several editions. He emphasized Serra's personal piety, holiness, and fierce dedication to the missions. Serra loved the Natives, he wrote, and they loved him.

Zephyrin Engelhardt, born in Germany, wrote a four-volume work, *Missions and Missionaries in California*. He glorified the sacrifices of the missionaries, but he regarded the Indians as "among the most savage, filthy, lazy, and improvident aborigines of America."

Maynard Geiger was a resident historian and archivist at Mission Santa Barbara. He wrote *The Life and Times of Fray Junípero Serra* (1959), a definitive biography of the Spanish friar, based on decades of research.

My former professor Francis Guest received his doctorate in history from the University of Southern California and spent years poring over archives in Mexico, Spain, and France. Guest published his findings in his book *Hispanic California Revisited* (1996), taking strong exception to criticisms of corporal punishment and forced conversions. Guest compared the floggings to "parent spankings" and suggested that the Indians willingly accepted the beatings "because they unified them with the sufferings of Christ." I once asked Guest to explain the conflict between the Indians and the friars. He responded casually, "Well, you talk with the Natives, you get one story, and with the friars, another."

The colonial narrative of the missions would not be complete without mentioning author and activist Helen Hunt Jackson. She admired the Franciscans and wrote *Ramona*, a romantic novel depicting mission life. It is still presented as a pageant play annually in Riverside County. Later she wrote *A Century of Dishonor*, which urged the US Congress to respect treaties with Indian nations.

Sherburne F. Cook, a University of California, Berkeley, physiologist, wrote *The Conflict between the California Indian and White Civilization* (1943). This was among the first major books to counter the traditional settler-colonial portrayal of the California missions. He drew from social sciences rather than from religious sources. His work examined life at the missions, including population decline, diseases, forced labor, and corporal punishment. Cook's writings upset Serra devotees, but historian Carey McWilliams supported the thrust of Cook's work with this comment: "With the best of intentions, the Franciscan padres eliminated Indians with the effectiveness of Nazis running concentration camps."

As seminary students, we were unaware of these polemics. We were spoon-fed the settler-colonial narrative through mimeographed notes. We told the tourists that the Chumash and other tribes were mere "diggers," existing at a very low level of civilization, and that the friars offered them a better life.

Our minds were colonized, and sadly, today's friars, too, seem uninterested in interrogating their assumptions about Serra and the missions.

THE FIRST PEOPLE

California Natives had lived here for thousands of years before the Spaniards "discovered" them. Most anthropologists believe their ancestors were Asians who migrated across the Bering Strait to Alaska. They lived in small family groups and were isolated by California's mountains and deserts from the more technologically developed tribes in the Great Plains.

In 1769, California Natives were a diverse population totaling some 300,000, which amounted to about 13 percent of the Indigenous people in North America. They spoke 136 dialects, and ranged from the Modoc tribe in northern California to the Maidu, Pomo Paiutes, and Ohlone in the central regions of the state to the Mojave, Chumash, and Kumeyaay in the south.

The California Natives were a large, healthy population with an ample food supply of grains and wild game, supplemented by plentiful fish from the sea and rivers. All that would change with the arrival of the Franciscans and Spanish soldiers in 1769.

Sadly, for many years the Natives weren't able to tell their stories. But they are doing so now and there is a marked change in today's scholarship and activism. That's always the result when people are able to tell their own stories—and the best is yet to come.

CHAPTER 8

What the Visitors Saw

I magine transporting yourself in a time machine back to the mission period (1769–1834). You would find the missions and their lands to be like crudely constructed labor camps, bustling with Native field hands, herders, and construction crews. Today, the missions function as Catholic retreat centers, seminaries, and parishes, with gurgling fountains and guided tours. Their reconstruction from adobe ruins began in the 1880s, when the railroads brought new settlers, land speculators, and tourists to the Golden State. Along with that came the revival of the fantasy heritage story that romanticized the missions as happy places where the friars and Natives toiled together in harmony.

But as has been noted, historical records, archives, and oral histories paint a different picture. My own method of approaching the missions is as a journalist, gathering information and drawing on the reflections of visitors such as Baron

Alexander von Humboldt and the French explorer Jean-Francois Galaup de Lapérouse.

In 1786, Lapérouse reported that the Indians at Mission San Carlos appeared "listless and depressed. They exhibit none of the love of independence and liberty that characterizes the nations to the north." He also remarked: "Corporal punishment is inflicted on Indians of both sexes who neglect exercises of piety. Many sins, which in Europe are left to divine justice, are here punished by irons and stocks." Noting the rigorous work schedule—seven hours of labor and two hours of prayer—Lapérouse observed, "The condition of the converted Indians scarcely differs from that of Negro inhabitants of our colonies, where we have seen both men and women in irons and stocks." Lapérouse also commented on Native child labor: "Many perish as a consequence of hernias. Our surgeons had the pleasure of relieving a small number and showing how to apply necessary bandages."

Seven years later, British explorer Captain George Vancouver remarked: "All the Indians' movements of both mind and body appear to be carried out with a mechanical, lifeless, and careless indifference." And thirty years after Lapérouse's visit, the Russian explorer Otto von Kotzebue offered a similar description of the Natives he saw at Mission Dolores: "A deep melancholy always clouds their face, and their eyes are constantly fixed on the ground."

In 1826, Captain Frederick William Beechey of England's Royal Navy described his visit to Mission San Jose. He attended a Mass with the Natives, heavily guarded by soldiers with fixed bayonets. "This congregation was very attentive," he said. "But the gratification they received from the music is proof of the strong hold these Romish ceremonies have upon their uninformed minds."

Among critics of the mission system was Scottish-born Hugo Reid. He arrived in California in 1837, married a Native woman from Mission San Gabriel, and received a land grant from the Mexican government. Reid was a gifted scholar, ethnographer, and writer, who recorded his findings on Native culture in a series of articles for the *Los Angeles Star* newspaper. Reid was sharply critical of Father Jose Maria Zalvidea's penchant for beating the Indians at Mission San Gabriel. He wrote in the *Star*: "When a woman was accused of infanticide for being pregnant with a 'white' baby, the padre had her punished by shaving her head, flogging her, and putting her into leg irons. He also ordered her to appear every Sunday near the steps to the altar with a hideous painted wooden child in her arms!"

PUSHBACK AGAINST THE SETTLER-COLONIAL NARRATIVE

Numerous scholars, including Native Californians, have criticized the Catholic Church and the Franciscan Order for spreading disinformation about the missions in general and Junípero Serra in particular. Professor Jonathan Cordero, formerly of California Lutheran University, has criticized two California archbishops for false and misleading statements about Junípero Serra, while repeating their own words: "Facts matter and the truth counts."

Cordero wrote in his personal blog: "The Catholic Church, not the activists, has rewritten the historical record to craft a fantasy heritage affirming racial, cultural, and religious superiority that maintains their economic and political privileges." Cordero argues that Serra's worthiness should be judged not by his intentions but by his policies as head of the mission. "Serra did not baptize or confirm any more Indians, nor did he found any more missions than any other missionary," he wrote.

Moreover, Cordero notes that the missions failed to realize their primary objectives: Genuine conversions did not occur for the majority of Indians, nor did the missions comply with Spanish law to produce self-governing settlements within ten years. Both Serra and his successor, Fermin de Lasuén, insisted that the Indians were not capable of such tasks. The results were disastrous for the Natives, who ended up as landless paupers.

In the wake of the Serra canonization, dissident groups began toppling statues of Saint Junípero Serra in the San Francisco Bay Area. Angered by the vandalism, Archbishop Salvatore Cordileone performed two exorcisms against "The Evil One," calling the acts blasphemous and sacrilegious. He also demanded that the Marin County district attorney press felony and hate crime charges against five Natives who felled the statues. As of this writing, the case is still pending in the court system. The Spanish missionaries believed the colonization of the Indians was a dramatic setting for a struggle between God and the Devil. Apparently, the archbishop believes Satan is still up to his old tricks.

As the mission period drew to a close in 1834, the Indians were forced into poverty and had to fend for themselves. Anthropologist Randal Milliken points out, the Natives did resist at times, but they were no match against the Spaniards' steel swords, muskets, and horses. They also faced high disease and mortality rates, oppressive working conditions, poor diets, and corporal punishments. Worst of all, the friars relentlessly campaigned to denigrate their cultural and religious practices. Fray Fermin de Lasuén put it succinctly: "They hear Mass daily, and those who accept the ten commandments are now convinced that it is right to punish them for their defects."

So yes, sins were committed during the colonization of California. But the question is, who was doing the sinning? And who was committing the crimes? That is the subject of the next chapter.

Mission San Diego de Alcalá. *GNU Free Documentation License.*

CHAPTER 9

Who Were the Real Sinners?

Valentin Lopez is the chairman of the Amah Mutsun tribal band, the people who originally populated Missions Santa Cruz and San Juan Bautista in Central California. He is heavyset, a passionate speaker, and constantly on the go, attending to the needs of his people. I first met him when Pope Francis announced his plan to canonize Fray Junípero Serra on September 23, 2015. Lopez was one of the first to speak out publicly against the event.

Lopez has a problem with the corporal punishment Serra and the friars enacted against the Natives when they left the missions without permission, engaged in promiscuous sex, stole what did not belong to them, or failed to attend Mass or prayer services.

I networked with his group of scholars and tribal leaders who opposed the canonization and sought to pressure the Catholic Church for accountability and a reckoning. Lopez, who was raised Catholic, discussed the concept of "sin" at a conference of scholars critical of the mission system (held July 15, 2020, at the Sycuan Casino conference room near San Diego). "Who were the sinners during the colonial period?" he asked. "It wasn't the Indians who committed the atrocities. That's for sure." Lopez relayed how his close friend Bishop Francis Anthony Quinn of Sacramento (1921–2019) told him that a true theology of evangelization should be based on the parable of the Good Samaritan. "You don't evangelize with swords and weapons," Quinn had told him, "but with kindness and generosity."

As the Serra canonization approached, Lopez, Quinn, tribal psychiatrist Donna Schindler, and several others wrote the Pope, asking him to cancel the canonization ceremony. He rejected their pleas, failing to respond to their several letters.

Now, almost a decade after the Serra canonization, relations between California Indians and the Catholic Church remain strained. Protests continue, but there is little movement toward the difficult dialogues that need to take place to air differences and to set realizable goals toward healing and reckoning.

There is no doubt that the church's theology of mission has changed dramatically since the Second Vatican Council (1962–65). It long ago renounced its ties with imperialism and colonialism, supplanting its former approach with concepts such as the preferential option for the poor, multiculturalism, and diversity.

Yet there is a finality with canonizations, crystallized in the expression *Roma locuta, causa finita* ("Rome has spoken, the issue is settled"). Nobody can be uncanonized. Nor can anybody measure the incalculable harm felt by Natives who continue to suffer intergenerational trauma from the mission period that enslaved their ancestors 250 years ago.

Scholars usually avoid theological topics and had some difficulty responding to Lopez's thoughts on sin. But he has spent a lifetime reflecting on this. He was raised Catholic and took the ten commandments seriously. He says the Bible helped him affirm what his parents taught him: to distinguish between right and wrong, good and bad, and to respect the rights of others. "It's basic stuff," he told me. "Like thou shalt not kill, thou shalt not commit adultery, and thou shalt not bear false witness against thy neighbor."

Lopez uses the word "sin" to describe the colonization process. It is not inappropriate to speculate that things could have turned out radically different had the friars simply invited the Natives to accept their religion without coercion, military bodyguards, guns, and body armor. The friars needed these things, ironically, to protect themselves from Indian reprisals after the soldiers raped Kumeyaay women and flogged their men. To this day, the docents at Mission San Diego tell tourists that the Kumeyaay attack was simply the work of two disgruntled Indians, not the rebellion of 700 fellow warriors. Serra asked for leniency for the culprits, an act that probably saved the future of the entire mission project.

As for who was committing the sins and the crimes at the missions, history will ultimately be the judge. But it is clear to me and many others that the Indians had nothing to do with it.

Mission San Luis Rey de Francia. *Creative Commons license.*

CHAPTER 10

~~~

What Do the Friars Say?

"I think many friars have had bad experiences with the media and don't trust them. They understand the complexities and abuses of colonialism, but in general most are comfortable with Pope Francis and the Serra canonization."—Friar Michael Guinan, Franciscan School of Theology, University of San Diego.

What do today's Franciscans think about Junípero Serra and the legacy of the twenty-one California missions? It's hard to know because so few friars are willing to speak about it, for a variety of reasons.

The mission period was controversial. It requires careful analysis and attention to new research. The archive at Mission Santa Barbara, where I studied theology, is the oldest library in California. It houses an enormous number of documents that describe every aspect of life at the missions, from the success of commercial ventures such as selling livestock and hides to traders from Europe to the suffering of Indians at the missions—all recorded in the friars' own words. The archivists never try to hide anything. It is there, most of it, in plain sight. Scholars have pored over thousands of pages of personal letters between the friars and government officials. The library is a treasure trove of information, and I am grateful for an opportunity to have studied in it. I have met scholars, Natives, and non-Natives there, all of whom have helped shape my perspective.

The process to canonize Serra—something much sought after by most Franciscans—began in the 1940s but stagnated due to a lack of miracles. Also, widespread community support failed to materialize. All that changed when Popes John Paul II and Francis decided to fast-track Serra's beatification and canonization. As Kenneth Woodward pointed out in his classic work, *Making Saints*, canonization is eminently a political process.

After two previous candidates failed the miracles test, Vatican medical officials approved the cause of Mother Boniface, a Franciscan nun in St. Louis who nearly died of a blood disease that was never diagnosed. She prayed to Serra and said her prayers were answered. Vatican medical experts claimed her cure was miraculous, because nothing else could explain her rapid recovery. Serra, they believed, was responsible.

Popes tend to put their fingers on the scale when looking for saintly role models. Mother Teresa was fast-tracked, and so was the authoritarian Pope St. John Paul II, to balance the canonization of the immensely popular St. Pope John XXIII, who called for the Second Vatican Council in the 1960s. This was to please both liberals and conservatives.

Father Ken Laverone was the vice-postulator for the Serra cause. I asked him if there were any plans for Masses of reconciliation with Native Californians, such as celebrated by Bishop Francis Quinn of Sacramento and Bishop Daniel Garcia of Monterey. He said, "Who knows? There might be." Nothing of the sort took place. Laverone appeared on the altar with Pope Francis at the canonization, flanked by two Catholic Indians who were his close friends.

I asked my classmate Ignatius de Groot, who retired as pastor of the San Carlos Apache Reservation east of Phoenix, what he thought of the Serra canonization. De Groot said Serra protected the Indians in a limited way, "but he was a part of Spanish culture that regarded the Indians as nothing. A saint, in the church's tradition, is someone to look up to and imitate. Serra was certainly not that."

The Serra beatification touched off a firestorm with Native Californians, who threatened to disrupt the ceremony in California. So instead, Serra was beatified at the Vatican in 1988. The bishop of Monterey chose the testimony of his own experts and stiff-armed Natives who opposed the beatification. He claimed their position was "poorly researched."

In a rush to canonize Serra, Pope Francis waived the second miracle required by Vatican protocols. He insisted that Latin Americans and US Latinos needed a role model and Serra was their man. Yet it was hard to detect any popular groundswell of support for Serra's canonization—certainly not from Native Californians. And I doubt very much that Mexicans, Puerto Ricans, or any other Hispanic group will light candles and pray to Serra. He is a distant figure to them.

Today, talk about healing, reconciliation, and reparations with Native Californians is still barely at the beginning stages. Recently, Governor Gavin Newsom apologized "for the exploitation and violence our predecessors inflicted upon them." He also promised to acquire and co-manage ancestral lands.

The friars do not all sing from the same choir, so to speak. Some simply do not care about the subject matter, leaving the details to the "experts." Others accept the findings of the hagiographers and refuse to accept the negative criticisms of Native scholars. The debate will continue.

There's more to this story. What do the Natives say? That is the subject of the next chapter.

CHAPTER 11

What Do the California Indians Say?

There is a reservoir of untapped oral histories among Native Californians about how their ancestors were treated at the missions. This history reaches back more than 200 years and became an issue in the mid-1980s when Pope John Paul II made plans to visit California to beatify Junípero Serra. Yet most historians seldom mention or access this history.

I learned this first-hand from my interviews with several Native Americans at a pow wow held in 2015 at Mission San Luis Rey near San Diego, where I had studied philosophy in the early 1960s as a young friar. The aroma of ceremonial sage brush and the sound of Indian drums and chants mingled with the cool ocean breeze blowing over the mission at the nineteenth annual Intertribal Pow Wow, described as a "celebration of history, culture, and spirit."

Hundreds of tribal members throughout the US attended the event and scores of visitors gathered in front of the picturesque mission. The main attraction was a large ceremonial circle, where Native Americans from throughout the US chanted and danced in colorful Native dress. Around the circle, tribal members from the Apaches, Kiowas, Navajos, Senecas, and other nations mingled with local Luiseño bands and Kumeyaays, sharing stories and comparing experiences and family memories. The upcoming canonization of Fray Junípero Serra was not a hot topic at the gathering, but most of the Indians I spoke with opposed it.

My particular focus that day was on the local Luiseño tribal members. I wanted to hear their stories. Carrie Lopez, a Luiseña council member, said that tribal members had mixed feelings about Serra and the missions. "We are very sophisticated Catholics," she told me. "We want to respect the pope, but we can't condone that shameful part of our history and the atrocities committed against our people."

Later, at a dinner in the mission quadrangle, council member Linda Fousset told me her family firmly opposed the canonization. "It upsets me," she said, tears welling up in her eyes. "I think of the beatings, and after the mission period, how Anglo settlers were paid five dollars for an Indian scalp."

Another Luiseña, who asked not to be identified, said her family had long ago abandoned Catholicism. "The church never did anything for our people," she said. "They destroyed our culture, our religion, and our way of life. And now they want us to thank them for this and canonize Serra. What's up with that?"

Edward Gonzales, also Luiseño, believed the canonization was purely political. "The church wants more members," he said. "Serra believed that all he did was for the benefit of the church. Our people believed in the Mother Earth, the sun, and the moon. Yet everything was taken away from them. Who gave them the right to do this?"

It has been more than nine years since Pope Francis canonized Junípero Serra. As noted previously, relations between Native Californians and the Catholic Church remain polarized, and talk of healing, reconciliation, and reparations with Native Californians has barely begun.

THE SERRA BEATIFICATION (1988)

As discussed in chapter 6, historians Rupert and Jeannette Costo (Cahuilla Luiseño) recorded the words of numerous Natives and tribal leaders concerning stories about Serra that had been passed down from their ancestors. But Bishop Thaddeus Shubsda of the Monterey diocese rejected these testimonies. Instead, he handpicked conservative scholars who supported the beatification. The beatification ceremony was moved from California to the Vatican because of the protests.

I also attended the 2019 Intertribal Pow Wow, and again interviewed several California Indians at the San Luis Rey Mission. Maurice Magante, a San Luis Rey descendant, told me his ancestors were forced to carry logs on their shoulders from Mount Palomar to Missions San Luis Rey and San Diego. "Our people were taken from their villages as slaves," he said. "We knew who we were, how to live, to care for the land and respect the rights and property of others."

"We had our own laws, our own civilization, and plenty of food," said Eva Kolb, also a San Luis Rey descendant. "The missions did no good for us, only harm. Why should Serra be called a saint? He may not have beaten us himself, but he ordered such things."

Lorena Dixon of the Pauma reservation told me, "The missionaries treated us like savages, like animals. To them we were pagans. They were cruel to our people, even to the kids. Many of us find it hard not to be against the missions, against Christianity."

Additionally, several tribal leaders condemned Bishop Shubsda's move. "To canonize a priest, no matter how pious, for acts that appear brutal, is not to be borne," said Banning Taylor of Los Coyotes Indian Reservation.

"The Viejas Band of mission Indians has known about the atrocities committed against Kumeyaay Tiipai people through the oral history of our people during the mission period. The Viejas tribal council designates Rupert Costo as a spokesman to correct the degrading statements made by Bishop Shubsda about California Indians," said Anthony Pico, tribal chairman.

The Costos published their findings and sent them to forty-five historians. Reactions ranged from disbelief and dismay to those who said the allegations were too ridiculous to bother with.

"Why bother?" Costo responded. "Because it concerns our people, our history, our ancestors, our religion, and our ancient beliefs. We are the original people of the land whose love for it and its creatures made it possible for other races to come here and make a good life for themselves and their children."

CHAPTER 12

The Lone Voice: Bishop Francis Quinn

It's no secret that Pope Francis' decision to canonize Fray Junípero Serra in 2015 received widespread support from US Catholic bishops, the Franciscan Order, the Knights of Columbus, and prominent US politicians.

Yet not everyone sang from the same choir. There was opposition, not only from the Native Californians and some scholars, as mentioned previously, but even from Francis Quinn, the retired bishop of Sacramento, California. Quinn was the sole outlier among the bishops, a lone voice who disagreed with the pope and pleaded with him to cancel the ceremony, which took place at the Shrine of the Immaculate Conception in Washington DC (see chapter 6).

Quinn took a keen interest in the plight of Native Americans, specifically the treatment they received during the Spanish colonization of California from 1769–1834. He believed the Franciscans, albeit with good intentions, did enormous harm to the Native population.

Quinn passed away at a Sacramento assisted-living center on March 21, 2019, at age 97. He was the oldest living Catholic bishop in the United States. Quinn was known as a critical thinker and caring pastor who supported the Gospel's preferential option for the poor. He frequently ministered to the homeless on the streets of Sacramento.

After he retired in 1993, he volunteered to work with Franciscan missionaries in Indigenous communities in Arizona. Quinn drove to Arizona in an RV camper gifted by the priests of Sacramento. He ministered to several reservations and parishes in the Tucson area: Tohono O'Odham, Yaquis, and Apaches.

"When I retired in 1993, I went to Tucson, Arizona, to work with the Tohono O'Odham people," he told me during a 2016 interview in Sacramento. He intended to do pastoral work there for one year, but stayed thirteen, saying Mass, baptizing, and doing counseling. "I worked with the Franciscans," said Quinn. "I've always been friendly with them. As for the Indians, at first they were shy, but once we got to know one another they were warm and affectionate."

Quinn told reporter Randy Pench that he was struck by the poverty he witnessed: "You could be in a ghetto or barrio in a large city," he said. "But what impressed me was the Native people's perseverance and strong family ties." Quinn frequently preached on family life. He told a congregation in South Tucson that he was raised in a single family home. He

Bishop Francis Quinn. *CNS/Courtesy Diocese of Tucson, Arizona.*

was six years old when his father died. "You can get along fine in a single parent family," he said.

Aware of the toll intergenerational trauma takes on Indigenous lives, Quinn composed his own "beatitude" that he shared with the Yaquis: "Blessed are families who seek to bring out the best in the other and who face their problems with a courageous spirit." Afterwards, several parishioners beat a small drum, singing a Mother Earth song. "I'm very comfortable with the bishop," said Ramona Valenta, a Tohono O'Odham woman who is part of the drum group. "He's very down to earth, humble, and connected to the people."

Quinn considers the Franciscans and other orders ministering to Native peoples as the real heroes. "They work with the people day and night, hour by hour," he told me.

When Quinn returned to California in 2006, he was invited to say a Mass to commemorate the founding of San Rafael Mission near San Francisco. In his homily he apologized to the Miwok Indians and decried the destruction of their spiritual practices and punishments at the hands of the Franciscans. "I've studied the Miwoks and I regret that they were treated unfairly," Quinn told the Catholic News Service. "They didn't expect an apology, so some of the Indians even wept. I looked upon it as a time of reconciliation." Greg Sarris, head of the Miwok tribal council, told the Associated Press that Quinn's remarks were "historic."

The Vatican has promoted an official biography of Junípero Serra by Rose Marie and Robert M. Senkewicz of Santa Clara University. In remarks to the press, Senkewicz adhered to the Vatican's narrative, saying that Serra had flaws, but that in the long run he was a saint who did more good than harm to the mission Indians.

Bishop Quinn expressed his disagreement with that position in letters to Popes Benedict XVI and Francis. In contacting the Vatican, Quinn worked closely with Dr. Donna Schindler, a California psychiatrist who works with Native tribes, and with Valentin Lopez, chairman of the Amah Mutsun tribal band, based in Central California. "We reached out several times to the popes, urging them not to canonize Serra, but all they did was offer us prayers," said Schindler, who specializes in intergenerational trauma. "Had they apologized, they would be forgiven. It would have been very healing."

Said Chairman Lopez, "We met with Bishop Quinn regularly. He referred to us as 'our team.' He said you don't evangelize with horses, weapons, armor, and aggression, but as the parable of the Good Samaritan. I loved that man."

As further scholarship reveals the depth of suffering caused by the colonization of Native Californians, there is a growing need for healing and reckoning. Francis Quinn dared to cross over, and used the power of his office to speak and search for the truth. May he rest in peace.

Mission Santa Barbara. *GNU Free Documentation License.*

CHAPTER 13

What Is the Role of Allies?

How does one become an ally to Indigenous people? An ally is a non-Indigenous person who seeks to make a commitment to understanding and undoing the harm done to Native peoples, their land, and their culture by colonization.

Indigenous people are sovereign nations who maintain a strong sense of self and kinship, as well as social and political traditions. They want non-Indigenous people to realize they are settlers. They want them to recognize the violent history of colonization, and that they continue to benefit from those injustices.

Settler culture stresses individual versus communal needs, capitalism as the unique means to meet material needs, and Christianity as the only moral authority. White supremacy and privilege are the products of settler colonialism.

Allies play a key role in supporting Native causes. Their numbers have grown and they have given valuable assistance in numerous projects such as land recovery, the revival of salmon runs in several rivers, and other projects. They do best when they get behind the Natives rather then try to lead them.

Sometimes allies cause problems. This happened with the protests against the Dakota Access Pipeline in South Dakota. Some who claimed to be allies were spies and agitators who were resentful and disruptive when told how to behave.

Put simply, allies need to listen more and talk less. Don't interrupt. Educate yourself to avoid offending people. Indigenous people need to lead the way. It's about equilibrium, not equality. You are going to make mistakes. Apologize and learn from your mistakes.

THE ROAD AHEAD

More than 240 years have passed since Spain completed its last colonial venture in California with the founding of the twenty-one Franciscan missions. The history was tragic for Natives. But despite incredible obstacles and setbacks, they have made a comeback, preserving their culture and increasing in numbers. California's Native population is currently the largest in the United States. Sixty-four percent were born in the state. The rest migrated from all over the United States with the passage of the Relocation Act of 1956.

This Native population rebound has occurred despite ignorant assumptions that Indian are extinct. The myth of extinction, as Native scholar Mali Obomsawin has said, is based on collective amnesia: "Ignorance protects us from shame, and denial bars us from problem solving."

Current population figures are all the more impressive when one considers the stunning decline of California's Native population from the founding of the missions in 1769 until 1900. When the Portola expedition arrived in what is now San Diego, there were approximately 300,000 Indians in California. By 1900, because of European diseases, overwork, and outright slaughter, the population declined to less than 25,000. Much is made about the planned genocide of Native Californians that began with the Gold Rush of 1849. In 1852, California Governor Peter Burnett declared open warfare against Native Californians, placing a bounty on Indian scalps and encouraging ranchers and miners to slaughter Indians.

In recent years, the Indigenous population has rebounded to more than 600,000, including those born in California and those from tribes from other states. It is proof that resistance, in its many forms, has allowed Natives to survive and prosper.

Nobody knows for sure with what shape the debate over reconciliation and reckoning will take place. Statues of Junípero Serra have been toppled from their pedestals along with mission bells, both seen as oppressive by Native activists. These protests are the work of small groups of protesters, but they raise public awareness. Most people are still influenced by the fantasy heritage of happy friars and contented Indians promoted by the Catholic Church. The truth needs to be told before change can take place.

ALLIES

Natives are capable of successfully fighting their own battles. I have witnessed this myself, having been personally involved in assisting some of their efforts. But they appreciate the support of strong allies, among them certain historians, journalists, and others who point out the lies and disinformation of their opponents.

There are many ways allies can help Natives. The first step is to understand their plight and become familiar with their history. Then search for ways to raise awareness and get involved.

If you live near a mission, take a tour. If you believe the information you hear is distorted or trivial, then discuss it with the docents. Write a letter to the pastor or administrator. Nothing will change unless complaints are made.

If you want to go further, contact a tribe in your area. Most have exciting development projects that need support. For example, the Amah Mutsun nation, located in Central California, is looking for volunteers to improve educational curriculum that accurately tells the story of the local missions.[9] Volunteers are needed at their Relearning Garden on the campus of UC Santa Cruz. The tribe also needs financial support to fund mental health projects. Their Humunya Foundation is a nonprofit under the Internal Revenue Code. All donations are tax deductible.

---

9. https://amahmutsun.org

If you live in the San Francisco Bay Area, you can contact Ohlone matriarch Corina Gould, who is a caretaker for the shell mounds, ancient burial sites for the ancestors.[10]

San Diego State University offers many opportunities for volunteers.[11] Additionally, you can contact the American Indian Resource Center in Los Angeles for information about volunteering.[12]

See the Resources section of this book for more examples of volunteerism. It is important to research the history of tribes in your area. Ask what type of support they need. Listen to their needs, which may involve pathways toward healthy food systems, land purchase assistance, and more.

Good luck!

---

10. https://bioneers.org/corrina-gould-and-the-ohlone-shell-burial-mounds-bioneers

11. https://newscenter.sdsu.edu/home/currentstudents.aspx9

12. https://lacountylibrary.org/american-indian-resource-center

Mission Carmel. *Creative Commons license.*

CHAPTER 14

~~~

Where Do We Go from Here?

Stanley Rodriguez, chairman of the Kumeyaay nation's Santa Ysabel tribal band near San Diego, speaks with an authoritative voice when he insists that his people have never surrendered and will keep resisting the colonization wrought by the missions. Rodriguez introduced me to Paul Cuero, a tribal elder at the Sycuan reservation. Cuero seemed very suspicious when he discovered I had been a Franciscan. Later, he told me his family stories, including the humiliations and even beatings that his mother experienced at the hands of the church.

It has been more than ten years since such stories inspired me to begin writing this book about the twenty-one California missions and the Franciscan friars. Those men crossed oceans, mountains, deserts, and plains to save the souls of "heathens" they believed needed evangelization and to bring them the benefits of European civilization.

Yet even today, the conventional settler-colonial narrative is never disputed by the docents at the missions, the friars themselves, nor the hierarchy of the Catholic Church. It has a firm grip on the imagination of most Californians and the state's commercial culture. Countless businesses, banks, and restaurants bear the mission brand.

Still, public awareness of the more factual counternarrative is gradually rising due to the efforts of several different groups.

THE SOCIAL SCIENTISTS

It wasn't until the twentieth century that both social scientists and Indigenous historians began to challenge the standard religious interpretations of mission history. The most prominent such figure is Sherburne Cook, a University of California physiologist whose book *The Conflict Between the California Indian and White Civilization* exposed mission history to stringent statistical analysis and indisputable factual data. This angered those who defended the padres, but it paved the way for other research from anthropologists, historians, and scientists.

INDIGENOUS SCHOLARS

Indigenous scholars have made significant inroads against the settler-colonial narrative. Perhaps the most prominent of these was Rupert Costo (1906–1989), of the Cahuilla nation, and his wife, Jeannette Henry Costo (1908–2001), a Cherokee, who were the founders of the American Indian Historical

Society. They produced a variety of books and publications on Native Americans and were effective as lobbyists for Indigenous issues. Yet they received little recognition in the wider academic community. Most regional and state historical conferences have until recently been dominated by conservatives, who favor the settler narrative, downplaying the role of Native Californians. The Costo Chair in American Indian Affairs at the University of California Riverside was named in Rupert Costo's honor. The Costos were Roman Catholics who staunchly opposed the beatification of Fray Junípero Serra.

In recent years there has been a spate of publications and books by Native American scholars about the missions. Jonathan Cordero (Chumash), a professor at California Lutheran University, has written extensive critiques of the Franciscans and the Catholic hierarchy for their defense of the Serra canonization. See also books by Tsim Schneider and Olivia Chilcote.

Steven Newcomb (Shawnee/Lenape) is the director of the Indigenous Law Institute and the author of *Pagans in the Promised Land: Decoding the Doctrine of Christian Discovery*. He frequently comments on issues related to the missions.

Debora Miranda (Ohlone/Costanoan) is the author of *Bad Indians: A Tribal Memoir*. During her career as a tribal leader, teacher, and writer, she has been an outspoken and articulate critic of the California mission system. She was one of the first tribal leaders to protest the canonization of Fray Junípero Serra. Miranda writes that the state-mandated Mission Project for California fourth graders to construct mission models "drain[s] the missions of their brutal and bloody pasts for popular consumption. Too often the lesson is about imperialism, racism, and Manifest Destiny rather than a jumping off point for critical thinking."

THE CURRENT SITUATION

It has been more than 255 years since Junípero Serra, Spanish colonists, and leather-jacketed Spanish soldiers planted their flag and a crude wooden cross on a beach in what is now San Diego, claiming it as a possession of the Spanish government.

Native Californians hold diverse views about Serra, the missions, and the friars. Some cling to the cultural and religious practices of their ancestors, while others embrace a variety of faiths, including agnosticism and atheism. Some are angry and defiant, while others seem apathetic and see the issue as irrelevant. Understandably, they focus instead on their immediate needs: federal recognition of their tribes, the restoration of their lands lost through broken treaties, disenrollment controversies with Indian casinos, and public health issues, such as domestic violence and femicide.

Meanwhile, some tribes have made progress in reclaiming rivers and lands that were lost, often partnering with nonprofit groups. The Yokuts, for example have recovered the Klamath river, which contains several important species of fish and wildlife. And Land Veritas, a California-based bank, has donated 500 acres to the Tataviam nation in Northwestern Los Angeles County. "This is the first such donation in a century," said Tataviam tribal chairman Rudy Cervantes. Tataviam territory originally occupied more than 1.5 million acres, from the mountains to the Pacific ocean.

Much progress in recent years is due to a new openness about the past from the state of California, and an apology issued by Governor Gavin Newsom. "I am sorry I knew so little about his," Newsom told a group of tribal leaders in 2018, referring to the atrocities and massacres committed against the Natives over a period of 100 years. "It was genocide, pure and simple," he added.

It is hard to forecast what the future brings. It is doubtful that the friars will engage in any meaningful dialogues with Indian tribes. Nor is it likely that either the Vatican or California bishops will change their opinions about Serra and the missions.

The time is ripe for a full-throated response by tribal leaders to Governor Gavin Newsom's apology. Compensation for the suffering and losses of the tribes since 1769 is long overdue. The Franciscans and the Catholic dioceses should hand over the titles to the missions to local tribes, for a starter. And Natives should be the ones telling their own stories, not others for them.

It is my hope that this book will shed light on this debate and lead to meaningful dialogue with all parties. I welcome your responses.

Group portrait of about thirty Franciscan friars outside
at Mission Santa Barbara, 1904. *Public domain.*

Conclusion

John Lennon's song "Imagine" stands out as one of his greatest hits because it expressed a collective need for people to come together in the face of the social strife and divisions that shook the United States in the 1960s.

Imagination provides a wellspring of possibilities that infuse every aspect of our lives. We see it when a child blows out the candles on a birthday cake; when filmmakers and actors produce amazing films; when newlyweds take off on their honeymoon, their car festooned with balloons and best wishes.

For the Christian colonizers of early California, there was no place for imagination because they regarded Native religious beliefs, rituals, dances, and culture as superstition and the work of Satan. The Natives' only hope for salvation, the friars believed, was baptism. Thus Indigenous Californians became second-class Spanish citizens, destined to serve as the workforce to build the future state of California.

Imagine if the Spanish government and the Franciscans had respected the Laws of the Indies, which stipulated that after ten years Native Californians were to take over governance of the twenty-one missions and make them self-sustainable. Imagine, if you will, the Franciscans handing over the titles of the missions to tribal councils, jointly administered with the collaboration of local bishops and military commanders.

But, tragically, there was no such imagination. The Native Californians were decimated, their cultures all but destroyed. Then, after secularization, the friars went back to Mexico and Spain, and both the Mexican and later the American governments let the missions fall into ruins. It wasn't until the 1920s that the state of California revived the concept of El Camino Real, the King's Highway.

This controversy is not going away. Hopefully, there will be more soul searching, accountability, and reckoning, so that the Franciscans, the Catholic Church, and Native leaders can come together for some meaningful closure. This may take time and patience, but it is well worth the effort.

As Kumeyaay tribal chairman Stanley Rodriguez stated several years ago during a conference at UC San Diego in La Jolla, "They came to steal our souls, our bodies, and our lands. We have never been conquered. We fought back from the beginning until today, and we will fight back forever."

Timeline of the Spanish Conquest of the Americas

1492: Christopher Columbus arrives on the Island of Hispaniola. His soldiers demand gold from the Arawak Indians. Hundreds of thousands of Natives perish in subsequent years. Indigenous people today no longer regard Columbus as a hero. Columbus Day has now become Indigenous' Peoples Day.

1531: Fray Juan de Zumárraga, Mexico's first bishop, spreads the story of the Virgin of Guadalupe, whose cult has unified Mexico's diverse Indigenous population.

1598: Conquistador Juan de Oñate enters New Mexico and sets up the European system of feudalism. He captures the Zuni village of Acoma and cuts off the right feet of male captives. The king revokes his charter. He is sent to Mexico City and tried for what we now call crimes against humanity.

1680: The Pueblo revolt. New Mexico pueblos revolt and drive the Spanish out of New Mexico. But in 1692, Don Diego de

Vargas leads a force of 60 Spanish soldiers and 100 Indian allies to reconquer New Mexico.

1767: The Jesuit order is expelled from all its colonies because of their conflicts with European monarchs and their accumulation of wealth and power. Their missions are handed over to the Franciscans.

1769: Fray Junípero Serra arrives with the Portola expedition to Upper California and plants the flag of Spain, establishing Mission San Diego, the first of twenty-one missions. Serra would go on to found eight more missions.

1775: Six hundred Kumeyaay warriors, angered by the abuses of Spanish soldiers, burn down Mission San Diego, killing its pastor, Fray Luis Jayme, and a blacksmith. Native rebellions later took place at Missions Santa Barbara, Ventura, La Purisima, and San Gabriel.

1821: Mexico, following the example of the thirteen New England colonies, wins its independence from Spain. The California missions are secularized in 1834 and the remaining friars return to Spain and Mexico.

1846: The US invades Mexico and takes over half its territory by force of arms The spoils are divided up in the 1848 Treaty of Guadalupe Hidalgo. Mexicans become foreigners in their own land, the American Southwest. Native Californians are dispossessed of their lands and condemned to poverty.

1849–1852: Gold is discovered in California, and the US Army invades and claims the state of California. Mexicans and Native Californians have no rights and are driven off their lands. In 1849, Peter Barnett is elected as the state's first governor. A white supremacist, he places a $5 bounty on Indian scalps and supports massacres against Indian villages.

1851–52: The California legislature signs treaties with eighteen Indian nations, whose holdings encompass 11,700 square miles. Despite its promises, the State of California never ratifies the treaties.

1891: The state offers certain tribes $150,000 for a few rancherias. The rest of the land is sold to private citizens. The Natives are condemned to lives of poverty and destitution.[13]

---

13. Source: Elisa Miller, state archivist.

Timeline of the Founding of the Twenty-One California Missions

1. Mission San Diego de Alcalá (1769)
2. Mission San Carlos Borromeo de Carmelo (1770)
3. Mission San Antonio de Padua (1771)
4. Mission San Gabriel (1771)
5. Mission San Luis Obispo de Tolosa (1772)
6. Mission San Francisco de Asís (Mission Dolores) (1776)
7. Mission San Juan Capistrano (1776)
8. Mission Santa Clara de Asís (1777)
9. Mission San Buenaventura (1782)
10. Mission Santa Barbara (1786)
11. Mission La Purisima Concepción (1787)
12. Mission Santa Cruz (1791)
13. Mission Nuestra Señora de la Soledad (1791)
14. Mission San José (1797)
15. Mission San Juan Bautista (1797)
16. Mission San Miguel Arcángel (1797)

17. Mission San Fernando Rey de España (1797)
18. Mission San Luis Rey de Francia (1798)
19. Mission Santa Inés (1804)
20. Mission San Rafael Arcángel (1817)
21. Mission San Francisco Solano (1823)

Resources

BOOKS

A Cross of Thorns: The Enslavement of California's Indians by the Spanish Missions, by Elias Castillo, Craven Street Books, Fresno, 2015. An important book that separates facts from fiction and fantasy.

The Conflict between the California Indian and White Civilization, by Sherburne F. Cook, University of California Press, Los Angeles, 1976. A definitive book on the colonization of California as opposed to the hagiography of previous books. Cook tells what really happened, using the tools of the social sciences.

Indians, Franciscans, and Spanish Colonization: The Impact of the Mission System on California Indians, by Robert H. Jackson and Edward Castillo, University of New Mexico Press, Albuquerque, 1996. This book debunks the fantasy heritage of the missions promoted by the Catholic Church.

Missionary Conquest: The Gospel and Native American Genocide, by George Tinker (Osage Nation), Fortress Press, Minneapolis, 1993. An excellent study of colonizers, both Catholic and Protestant.

An Indigenous People's History of the United States, by Roxanne Dunbar Ortiz, Beacon Press, Boston, 2014. The author gives a detailed history of the Doctrine of Discovery.

Open Veins of Latin America: Five Centuries of the Pillage of a Continent, by Eduardo Galeano, Monthly Review Press, New York, 1973. A classic work about Spain's conquest of Latin America.

American Holocaust: The Conquest of the New World, by David Stannard, Oxford University Press, 1992. A definitive work on colonialism in Latin America.

Southern California: An Island on the Land, by Carey McWilliams, Peregrine Smith, 1946.

Junípero Serra: California, Indians, and the Transformation of a Missionary, by Rosemary Beebe and Robert Senkewicz, University of Oklahoma Press (in cooperation with The Academy of American Franciscan History), Norman Oklahoma, 2015. This book was funded by the Franciscan Order.

We Are the Land: A History of Native California, by Damon B. Akins and William J. Bauer Jr., Oakland, University of California Press, 2021.

Resurrecting the Past: The California Mission Myth, by Michelle Lorimer, Great Oak Press, Pechanga, California, 2016. There were two beginnings, first in 1769, then again in the 1880s, when the missions were restored as tourist attractions.

Native Americans of California and Nevada, by Jack Forbes, Nature Graph Publishers, Happy Camp, California, 1982.

Junípero Serra: California's Founding Father, by Steven Hackel, Hill and Wang, New York, 2013.

A Violent Evangelism: The Political and Religious Conquest of the Americas, by Luis N. Rivera, John Knox Press, Louisville, 1990.

Making Saints: How the Catholic Church Determines Who Becomes a Saint, Who Doesn't, and Why, Kenneth L. Woodward, Simon and Schuster, 1990.

The Archives of Mission Santa Barbara, the oldest library in California. Open to scholars by appointment only. Address: 2201 Laguna St., Santa Barbara, CA 93105. (805) 682-4713, ext. 152.

ADDITIONAL RESOURCES

For fourth graders: https://www.zinnedproject.org/if-we-knew-our-history/california-missions-and-indians.

The California Native American Heritage Commission (NAHC), created in statute in 1976 (Chapter 1332, Statutes of 1976), is a nine-member body whose members are appointed by the Governor. The NAHC identifies, catalogs, and protects Native American cultural resources—ancient places of special religious or social significance to Native Americans and known ancient graves and cemeteries of Native Americans on private and public lands in California. The NAHC is also charged with ensuring California Native American tribes' accessibility to ancient Native American cultural resources on public lands, overseeing the treatment and disposition of inadvertently discovered Native American human remains and burial items, and administering the California Native American Graves Protection and Repatriation Act (CALNAGPRA), among many other powers and duties. https://nahc.ca.gov/calnagpra

The American Indian Reporter: This website has news, resources, and opportunities for volunteers. www.california-indianeducation.org

The East Bay shellmound and Ohlone matriarch Corina Gould: bioneers.org/corrina-gould-and-the-ohlone-shell-burial-mounds-bioneers.

News from Native California: a quarterly magazine with news, poetry, art, and tribal histories of Native California. newsfromnativecalifornia.com

Indian Country Today (ICT), a great source of news on Native Americans. https://ictnews.org

American Indian Education Centers (California Department of Education): www.cde.ca.gov/sp/ai/re/aidirectory.asp

Acknowledgments

My thanks to many people, Natives and non-Natives, who have helped me understand the California missions, where I lived and studied as a Franciscan friar in the 1960s.

I am grateful to several scholars, including Valentin Lopez, chairman of the Amah Mutsun tribal band in Central California. Lopez has challenged the Serra canonization and the settler-colonial narrative of the Catholic Church and the Franciscan Order. And he has always done so respectfully.

I am thankful as well to Steve Newcomb, author of *Pagans in the Promised Land*, for his profound analysis of the Doctrine of Discovery.

The result of the Spanish colonization of California, as Lutheran theologian George "Tink" Tinker (Osage) points out, was the destruction of Indigenous people's religion and their family ties, and the loss of their land. His short book *Missionary Conquest: The Gospel and Native American Cultural Genocide*, belongs in the library of anyone interested in the California missions.

I am also indebted to the Critical Mission Studies program, organized by University of California scholars. I thank

Jennifer Hughes of UC Riverside for welcoming me into this group of distinguished scholars and for encouraging me to write this book.

My special thanks to Professor Jonathan Cordero of California Lutheran College, who stands out with his perceptive critiques of the settler-colonial narrative, the Catholic hierarchy, and the Franciscan Order. I met him at the Santa Barbara mission archives and I appreciate his valuable input whenever I call upon him for advice.

Thank you to Jonathan Jaramillo, who frequently lent his considerable computer skills to me as I wrote and organized this manuscript, for which I am tremendously grateful.

I am indebted to Kent Sorsky, my editor at Linden Publishing. He believed in this book and encouraged me to dig deep and cover all the bases as accurately as possible. He filled in context and provided smooth transitions where needed, making the book very readable. He did a terrific job, for which I am very grateful.

Special thanks to Wayne Reese, who provided valuable assistance in researching photos and other data for this project. He helped make it a better looking book.

I thank Caroline Ward for her pilgrimage to all twenty-one missions, exposing what her ancestors went through, including the humiliation of being buried in unmarked mass graves.

Rupert Costo and Jeannette Costo were founders of the American Indian Historical Society. They led the opposition to the Serra beatification by Pope John Paul II. Their work is invaluable.

Acknowledgments

I regret the passing of journalist Elias Castillo (1939–2020), author of *A Cross of Thorns*. He was a good friend whose groundbreaking scholarship on the enslavement of California Indians is a major contribution to mission studies.

Special thanks also to Dr. Jeremiah Sladeck of UCLA, who shared his extensive research on the Franciscan missionaries and their epic struggle with military governors. I am also indebted to Julia McClure, author of *The Franciscan Invention of the New World*, which traces the conflicted and complex history of the Franciscan Order in Latin America.

Francis Guest, OFM, my church history professor at Mission Santa Barbara, was an excellent teacher but a strong defender of Serra and the mission system.

Another confrere, Maynard Geiger, founded the history archives at Mission Santa Barbara, the oldest and most complete collection of mission history. Though Geiger strongly supported the Serra canonization, his work as an archivist opened the gates to a treasure trove of documents for all scholars.

I am indebted to several other scholars. Steve Hackel of UC Riverside stands out with his encyclopedic knowledge of Serra and the missions. I also received help from James Sandos of the University of Redlands, who wrote extensively on the conversion of the Indians.

I am also grateful to historian Dr. Clifford Trafzer of UC Riverside. His editorial comments and suggestions have been extremely valuable.

And finally, I appreciate the critical comments and suggestions of Mike Connolly (Kumeyaay Tiipaay), whose knowledge of his people I highly respect.

Above all, I am grateful to my Indigenous brothers and sisters. They suffered many wrongs historically, and those wrongs need to be righted.

I hope this short book will help tell their story.

Respect for them is long overdue.

Index

Index

Index

Index

About Mark Day

Born in San Francisco, Mark Day is a practicing Roman Catholic and a former Franciscan priest. He spent twenty-two years with the order: first as a high school seminarian in Santa Barbara, and then at San Luis Rey College, where he received his bachelor's degree in philosophy. He then completed his studies at the Franciscan
School of Theology in Santa Barbara and was ordained a priest in 1965. After working in the pastoral ministry for ten years, he left the priesthood, having received a dispensation from Pope Paul VI.

Day subsequently earned masters degrees in journalism and professional writing at the University of Southern California and taught community college journalism for ten years. Later he covered the West Coast for the *National*

Catholic Reporter and served as a freelance reporter in Peru for five years.

Day has written and produced several award-winning documentaries on culturally diverse films, from chemical poisoning and polluted rivers on the US/Mexico border to the story of Irish immigrants caught up in the turmoil of the US intervention in Mexico (1846–47). He is a frequent contributor to the *National Catholic Reporter, Indian Country Today*, and other publications. He is the author of *Forty Acres: Cesar Chavez and the Farmworkers* (Praeger, 1971).

Day's views on the California missions have evolved over the years, and this short book reflects that analysis. He believes it will contribute to the ongoing debate between Indigenous Californians, the friars, and the Catholic Church.

You can contact Mark Day at Mday700@yahoo.com.